D0617135

Jimmy Evans has a clear message about marriage and sexuality that the entire world needs to hear. He cuts through the confusion with practical revelation and insight that is so desperately needed today.

Brady Boyd
Senior Pastor, New Life Church
Colorado Springs, Colorado

In a culture where sex and sexuality are completely misunderstood, maligned and misused, we need a clarion call. Jimmy Evans provides just that in this incredible new book. Read it for yourself and then become a part of the movement to defend, redeem and promote one of God's most precious gifts and creative expressions.

Alan Chambers
President, Exodus International

Sex is God's territory, and it's time Christians unashamedly took it back! With this book, Jimmy Evans will help you unveil the Deceiver's lies about sex so that you can experience God's best in your marriage. In Christ, the gift of sex is ours to cherish. This book will show you how.

Ron L. Deal
President, Successful Stepfamilies
Author, *The Smart Stepfamily*

In *The Fig Leaf Conspiracy*, Pastor Jimmy Evans masterfully pulls back the covers to expose the very core of the devil's strategy of deception to pervert God's gift of sexuality to His creative beings. Jimmy arms his readers with powerful Scriptures and godly advice while exposing the truth behind the master conspirator's plan of destruction, sin, deception and confusion.

Marcus D. Lamb
Founder and president, Daystar Television

Jimmy Evans has done it again! His message to all of us is that God created sex. It truly is His idea! And in our culture, our flesh and in the midst of the spiritual warfare for our souls, we need a biblical response. Jimmy gives us a biblical response to understanding God's design for a great sexual relationship within marriage. Read this book and pass it on to someone you care about! We will!

Dr. Gary and Barb Rosberg
Authors, *The Five Sex Needs of Men and Women*
Radio program co-hosts, *Dr. Gary and Barb Rosberg, Your Marriage Coaches*

Having grown up in a totally dysfunctional environment, I know first-hand that only God, through His divine guidance and the truth of His Word, can lead people out of the darkness produced by negative sexual influences. God has given Jimmy Evans the insight to offer meaningful and effective direction in this critical area of need.

James Robison
Founder and president, LIFE Outreach International
Fort Worth, Texas

jimmy evans

[revealing] s e x u a l i t y

as it was meant to be

the fig leaf
conspiracy

Regal

From Gospel Light
Ventura, California, U.S.A.

Published by Regal
From Gospel Light
Ventura, California, U.S.A.
www.regalbooks.com
Printed in the U.S.A.

Library of Congress Cataloging-in-Publication Data
Evans, Jimmy.
The fig leaf conspiracy / Jimmy Evans.
p. cm.
ISBN 978-0-8307-4532-6 (hard cover)
1. Sex—Religious aspects—Christianity. I. Title.
BT708.E93 2007
241'.66—dc22
2007034010

1 2 3 4 5 6 7 8 9 10 / 10 09 08

Rights for publishing this book outside the U.S.A. or in non-English languages are administered
by Gospel Light Worldwide, an international not-for-profit ministry. For additional information,
please visit www.glww.org, email info@glww.org, or write to Gospel Light Worldwide,
1957 Eastman Avenue, Ventura, CA 93003, U.S.A.

Contents

Part III:
the conspiracy unfolds

Part IV:
the conspiracy undone

Part V:
the keys to sexual fulfillment
in marriage

foreword

One of the most enjoyable things I do is introduce wonderful people to other wonderful people, and it's what I'm doing now.

"How do you know I'm wonderful, Jack?" you may be asking yourself. "You sound like you're laying a 'schmooze job' to me." But listen, please. I'm not "shining you on" or guilty of "schmoozing" you.

To begin, I know something about you already, simply by reason of the fact that you've picked up this book. You're curious—at the very least, inquisitive about the unusual title on the cover—and that alone is a kind of "wonder-full-ness": You wondered about this.

But that justification for my description of you as "wonderful" is only technical—only the result of a definition—less than a personal description rooted in some familiarity or relationship. So let me go to the real reason I believe you are "wonderful."

You're human. You were created on purpose, not born as an accident. Irrespective of your personal history or your parentage, whether you were planned or not, there is someone who thought of, planned for, and presently thinks very much of you. That someone is God!

And, mentioning Him, let me curb any inclinations you may have to doubt that fact. If any influences have reduced your confidence in His reality, His love or His truth, it's time to give Him a chance to reveal to you the magnificence and genuineness of Himself. And I can't think of a better way to begin understanding what God is really like than in reading this book.

This is a book about sex.

Maybe your jaw just hit the floor: "God? Sex? And in the same paragraph?!" In response, I say: Yes, absolutely! Not only because everything good about our human sexuality was invented by Him, but also, moreover, because He truly intends for us to each find the way to that relationship that introduces the possibilities of the highest, most continual fulfillment that our sexual capacities can bring! We are "wonderfully made," the Bible says—and that's just another reason I have to legitimize describing you as "wonderful," though we've probably never met.

Which, having said, brings me to saying something about the other "wonderful person"; for, as I said at the beginning, I'm only here at the beginning of this book to launch you forward, and that means introducing you to Jimmy Evans.

There are thousands upon thousands of people who would say this: Jimmy Evans is a wonderful speaker, teacher and communicator! I am one of those who would lead that cheer and do so with no hesitation because once anybody encounters him—in a seminar, on a telecast, recorded on a CD or DVD—they inevitably say something like, "Terrific!" But even better than that, they say, "Wow, that's clearer than I've ever heard anything like that before!"

The "that" they are usually referring to most often has something to do with issues practical to our daily life. Jimmy helps people think clearly about life—and that's enough to occasion saying anyone is "wonderful."

One more thing, and then I'm done with this introduction. Stay with me.

It isn't Jimmy Evans's remarkable communication skills that most impress me. It's his character and the way he lives out his commitments. While Jimmy is a pastor and a Bible teacher, his credibility isn't the result of an obligation to his profession, however right such a sense of duty is. It is born of conviction—non-religious (refreshingly real), non-prudish (often hilariously funny and always transparently forthright), and non-stodgy (keeping you alert, intent, and mixing laughter with rich discovery—always).

Jimmy has brought these qualities to his marriage of 34 years to Karen, his lovely wife. And it is from the context of their growth as a couple, as friends and as lovers, that he brings such a wealth of practical and penetrating insight as you'll find here.

So open the following pages and be enriched. Be drawn from the impoverished confusion of a society that is sexually tormented at the same time it has claimed to be so liberated. And let your eyes—more, your heart and mind—feast on truth that unleashes from chains of whatever confusion, disappointment, deadliness or shame "sex" has brought or dealt to you.

There's something wonderful here! And I'll tell you now—the wonder and fulfillment our Creator always intended you to find is closer than ever because you have this book in hand.

Dr. Jack W. Hayford
Chancellor, The King's College and Seminary
Founding Pastor, The Church On The Way

PART I

the conspiracy
is conceived

CHAPTER 1

in the beginning

A very long time ago, in a land far away, there lived God's beloved children, Adam and Eve. Life was good—they had everything anyone could ever want and they enjoyed an amazing relationship with God and with each other.

So how could they fall prey to temptation—when they had it all? The answer: The devil is the best con man around. He made them think they were lacking something—when in fact they weren't. If they had spent a moment to reflect, they would have seen through the deception. But they didn't. And in a single act of disobedience, they forfeited God's gifts—among which was their harmonious sexual relationship with each other.

The Loss

Lucifer paced back and forth on a high ledge overlooking the perpetual fires. Smoke billowed round about as intermittent light from the flames flickered in the darkness. His twisted mind was grinding on a plan for *revenge*. That's what he craved.

Banished from heaven by God, humiliated before the heavenly hosts and reduced to living in this place of torment, Lucifer was determined to find a way to strike back. The plan of attack would have to be perfectly crafted and devastatingly deceptive. He knew this called for a *conspiracy*—a skillful plot that could be carried out covertly. That was the only way to get to the Creator. All too well Satan knew God's power was superior to his—it was a fact he had learned the hard way.

Satan knew he could not attack the Creator directly. He would have to be cunning. Mid-stride, he stopped as the thought struck him: *If I hurt what He loves, I hurt Him!* He had seen the Creator walk and talk with the man and woman in the Garden. Lucifer knew how much God loved these beings—and he couldn't stand it. He couldn't bear the fact that these mere humans were the object of God's affection. For a moment, he remembered how beautiful his own life had been in heaven. *They live in Paradise, a place like heaven, while I live in the shadows and darkness! They have a relationship with the Creator unlike any other.* He seethed with resentment.

He knew now what he wanted to do, but the question was how to do it? Lucifer knew he had no creative power of his own. He did, however, possess an extraordinary ability to deceive. It was a skill so highly developed that he had managed to persuade a full third of the angels to follow him in his foolish rebellion. Yes, somehow he would have to deceive Adam and Eve into giving their world to him.

He had the right approach—he knew it. *I will control and ultimately destroy the man and woman,* he thought. *Disfigure the creation and the Creator will grieve!*

He had noticed that the couple had been given a wondrous way to fulfill God's purposes: their sexuality. To that end, the Creator had given them a gift that bound them together in a covenant unlike any other. At the same time, this gift gave the couple great pleasure, joy and deep intimacy. Pondering all of this produced a flash of twisted inspiration. Suddenly, he knew exactly how he could interfere with their relationship with the Father and their love for each other. He was especially interested in achieving this because he understood how much the Father delighted in knowing that Adam and Eve enjoyed all He had done for them.

"I'll go after the gift too," the devil muttered under his vile breath. "I'll separate them from each other and the Father, and steal this precious gift. Their lives will be as miserable as mine when they lose their place of favor with Him."

His objective was clear, and he plotted and conspired until he knew just the way to do it.

The day of opportunity finally came. Eve was alone. It was time.

The devil slithered into the Garden and implemented his plan *flawlessly*. The woman had no idea the harmless-looking being with the soft, enticing voice had anything other than her best interest at heart.

He was expertly cloaked in deception. Under a cover of flattery and lies, the enemy of the Father stealthily entered Adam and Eve's world. He convinced this naive couple to accept his version of the truth rather than the Father's word. He was subtle in his approach—Adam and Eve never dreamed this seemingly harmless serpent was the father of lies. In fact, they were completely astonished when he succeeded in bringing such a terrible curse into their lives and beautiful world!

This precious couple, who had enjoyed intimacy with each other and with the Father, now hid in shame. As the fearful man and woman covered their gift under fig leaves, hell celebrated. In that instant, the enemy was able to take control of the beautiful gift—and bring darkness, death and destruction into a perfect world that had been filled with light and life and love.

"I have won!" the devil crowed. "And it won't end here. Every person on Earth, and every marriage will suffer the effects of my deception. It will be one of the best tools in our arsenal against the human race. It is perfect!"

No sooner was the announcement made than the Creator came front and center. The devil cowered at the presence of Almighty God. He should have known the Father wasn't about to sit back and do nothing! Faster than he could comprehend, a plan was set in motion to undo his work of wickedness.

Because you have done this, [the Lord God thundered to the serpent] you are cursed more than all cattle, and more than every beast of the field; on your belly you shall go, and you shall eat dust all the days of your life. And I will put enmity between you and the woman, and between your seed and her Seed; He shall bruise your head, and you shall bruise His heel (Gen. 3:14-15).

The devil reeled under the weight of those words. He didn't fully understand the meaning, yet he knew that what God had declared was a terrible threat to his plan. Adam and Eve didn't understand it either. They didn't know God was sharing with them His plan of redemption— His plan to send Jesus into the world to restore what had been lost.

The Conspiracy Continues

God's promise to redeem humanity and the gift of human sexuality did not, however, prevent the serpent from continuing to implement his conspiracy. Adam and Eve had given him legal entrance into the earth— and access to humankind. He would use that advantage, and whatever time he had left, to work in the earth. To continue to pervert the gift of sexuality and destroy the lives of the children the Father loves so well.

Think I'm putting too much emphasis on this whole sex thing? Well, consider Adam and Eve's relationship before the Fall. Consider their view of themselves as sexual—they were not ashamed.

Then the rib which the Lord God had taken from man He made into a woman, and He brought her to the man. And Adam said: "This is now bone of my bones and flesh of my flesh . . ." And they were both naked, the man and his wife, and were not ashamed (Gen. 2:23,25).

Now, think about what came after. Shame. Disharmony in Adam and Eve's marriage. Pain in childbearing. Lack of unity between the sexes. Lust. Sin. You only have to read the Old Testament to see how God's children soon fell into sexual sin—everything from adultery to deviant behavior.

And they weren't the only ones. Generations of men and women from every country in the world have struggled—and continue to struggle—with all kinds of sex-related issues. Nonbelievers and believers alike suffer from a perverted view of sex and their own sexuality. Certainly the evidence indicates that Satan's deception in the Garden has been more effective and far reaching than any of his other schemes.

Down through the ages, the Fig Leaf Conspiracy has touched countless lives, including your own. Our loving Father, however, has made a way for us to be healed from its effects and to take back the precious gift of human sexuality—the way it was meant to be. He sent Jesus to undo the work of the deceiver. He has made a way of escape for us—a way back to the Garden.

truth in the garden

I have obviously used poetic license here in showing you the "behind the scenes" part of the familiar story of the Fall. Nevertheless, I think the picture I've painted accurately reflects spiritual reality and is supported throughout the Bible.

Scripture makes it clear that the enemy hates the Father and His children. He hates the fact that God not only gave Adam and Eve (and us as well) every provision, but that He also gave them the gift of sexuality, which was intended to bring tremendous blessings in their lives. The destruction and heartache the devil has brought upon humankind by stealing this gift cannot be overstated.

Since the Garden of Eden, the devil has used a perverted view of sexuality as a tool to deceive and shame men, women and children. In our present culture, the onslaught of sexual deception and temptation is greater than at any other time in history. You need only turn on the television and flip through the channels if you doubt that assertion.

So what is the answer? How do we get back to God's original plan for sexuality? By combating Satan's lies with God's truth as revealed in His Word.

Human Sexuality: God's Gift

So, that being said, let's dive into God's Word, where we find some powerful insights into God's design for sexuality. The second chapter of the book of Genesis describes how God created the woman and brought her to the man. It goes on to define their sexual relationship: "Therefore a man shall leave his father and mother and be joined to his wife, and they shall become one flesh. And they were both naked, the man and his wife, and were not ashamed" (Gen. 2:24-25).

Clearly God has designed a man and a wife to "be joined" to each other in the unique covenant bond of sexual union. In the Garden of Eden, before the fall of humankind, Adam and Eve were completely naked before each other—and completely *unashamed*. That was, and is still, God's intention for a husband and wife.

Genesis 1:31 also tells us, "Then God saw everything that He had made, and indeed it was very good." Notice that *everything* God made was very good. That description must include God's creation of sex and sexuality.

It is vitally important to understand that God created us to be sexual. It wasn't by accident. Sexuality was something He programmed in us for His highest purposes. He doesn't blush or frown in disgust when we talk appropriately about sex—or talk to Him about it. He is not embarrassed or ashamed when a married couple engages in sex. He is not disappointed in a husband and wife who enjoy physical intimacy. Quite simply, we are a sexual people because God made us to be that way. To be whole and free individuals, we must embrace this truth: Sex is an integral part of our makeup. And as such, it is also central to God's purpose for our lives.

This is why Satan's deception—and Adam and Eve's resulting sin—impacted human sexuality in such a devastating way:

So when the woman saw that the tree was good for food, that it was pleasant to the eyes, and a tree desirable to make one wise, she took of its fruit and ate. She also gave to her husband with her, and he ate. Then the eyes of both of them were opened, and they knew that they were naked; and they sewed fig leaves together and made themselves coverings (Gen. 3:6-7).

Only moments before eating the forbidden fruit, Adam and Eve had been naked and unashamed, just as God intended. But notice, as soon as they ate of the forbidden fruit, they felt ashamed of their sexuality. Their first instinct was to sew fig leaves together in an effort to hide their sexuality from each other and from God. The devil's first taste of victory came in twisting what God had declared to be "very good" and wrapping it in a mantle of disgrace.

God, however, is never ashamed of sexuality—remember, He is the One who created it! In fact, God wants us to enjoy the world He created. He wants us to have fun. It startles some Christians' religious sensibilities to think of God as "fun." But He is. That's why sex, expressed in accordance with God's plan and boundaries, is fun. It was God who thought it up!

Shame or Guilt—What's the Difference?

Since God will never shame us for being sexual or for being interested in sex, why is it that married believers so often feel ashamed of it? Where is this shame coming from? One source: the devil. In fact, *all shame of sexuality is demonic.* I realize that is a strong statement, but it follows logically once we recognize that shame of sexuality came as a result of the Fall—as a result of the devil's influence—not as a part of God's original creation.

Now, when I say all shame of sexuality is demonic, I am referring to shame about having sex *within God's design in the confines of marriage.* It would be appropriate to experience a righteous guilt or conviction about sexual sin. For example, a consumer of pornography ought to feel a healthy sense of "shame" about what he is doing because pornography is outside of God's design for sexuality.

Of course, the devil does *not* want anyone to feel ashamed for *sexual sin.* In fact, he works overtime to try to convince people that sexual sin such as adultery, pornography and homosexuality is acceptable (and movies, music and television all play a role in reinforcing this false message). The devil is trying his best to entice people to participate in sexual sin so that he has an opportunity to bring destruction—he is all for that!

The enemy only wants people to feel ashamed of sex when it is within God's plan and design—he desires to steal the joy of sex from married couples. His goal is to destroy lives and destroy marriages. Shame, which comes from the devil, is designed to push us away from God—to condemn us and leave us hopeless.

Shame is not a feeling about *what we have done*—rather, shame is focused on *who we are*. "Your sexuality is wrong," shame says, "and there is nothing you can do about it. There is something fundamentally wrong with the way you were created and you ought to be ashamed."

But shame needs to be distinguished from guilt, which is a normal healthy reaction we have when we directly violate God's command-ments. This conviction is the voice of conscience telling us something is not right. *That* is from the Holy Spirit and is designed to bring us to a point of repentance. Conviction for sin will draw us back into the light of God's love and His forgiveness.

Remember, God created our sexuality, and so even when we sin, He will never shame us about the way He created us. *Convict* us when we sin—*yes*. Shame or *condemn* us for who we are—*no*.

The Bible tells us, "There is therefore now no condemnation to those who are in Christ Jesus" (Rom. 8:1). The fact is that God sent Jesus not to condemn us, but that through Him we might be saved (see John 3:16). And Jesus cares about us so much, He sent the Holy Spirit into the world to be our Helper. He is here to help us live our lives God's way so that we can walk in the good things God has planned for our lives. He is here to help us know what is right and wrong—to convict us of sin, for our benefit (see John 16:7-8). Yet conviction from the Holy

Spirit always is loving and specific, and is designed to deliver us from sin and draw us to Jesus. Never does His conviction leave us without hope or condemned.

Fear Comes on the Heels of Shame

Shame and condemnation, as I've said, are from the devil and are designed to separate us from God. The enemy wants us to believe there is something wrong with us and with our sexuality. Sin brought *shame* and *condemnation* into this world, but those two never travel alone. Close on the heels of shame invariably come *fear* and *deception*. This is just what we see in the aftermath of the Fall:

> And they heard the sound of the Lord God walking in the garden of the cool of the day, and Adam and his wife hid themselves from the presence of the Lord God among the trees of the garden. Then the Lord God called unto Adam, and said to him, "Where are you?" So he said, "I heard Your voice in the garden, and I was afraid because I was naked; and I hid myself" (Gen. 3:8–10).

Until this point, Adam had lived before God without shame or fear. Why then was Adam suddenly hiding from God and quaking with fear? It might seem reasonable to assume Adam was afraid because he knew he had sinned against God. That, however, is not the case entirely. Out of his own mouth, Adam tells us the real reason behind his fear. He said, "I was afraid because I was naked." In Adam's thinking, being sexual was no longer normal, beautiful and good.

Notice, however, that the Creator wasn't satisfied with Adam's answer. He pressed the issue: "Who told you that you were naked? Have you eaten from the tree of which I commanded you that you should not eat?" (Gen. 3:11). In effect He was saying, "Why were you afraid because you were naked? Where did you get the idea that there is something wrong with your sexuality? That sort of idea did not come from Me. So, Adam, where did it come from?"

Now, of course God knew the devil was the originator of this idea—but did Adam know the perpetrator? I don't believe so. I suspect Adam had been deceived into thinking the shame and fear he felt was normal—somehow appropriate. After all, the very core of the devil's strategy is always deception, so it stands to reason the enemy would try to make Adam believe he (the devil) had nothing to do with the fear and shame Adam was feeling.

Part of the enemy's strategy is to use the same playbook he used with Adam—to conceal the very fact that we are being deceived by him. He subtly whispers lies. He covertly weaves doubts and shame into our thinking. We aren't consciously aware of what is taking place. But many people today are living in bondage because of this very strategy. They have no idea the devil has influenced their thoughts and opinions—they are unaware that he has been deceiving them and undermining God's plan for their lives.

Don't Buy the Lie

God is always trying to bring the truth to light. It was imperative for Adam to think about what had happened to him and to realize that when he had disobeyed God's command, a door to shame and deception was opened. God wanted Adam to understand that his disobedience had opened his mind to thoughts and ideas He never intended him to have.

The same thing is true in our lives. When we sin, we open wide a door for the devil to saunter in and begin to lie to and deceive us. His lies are against God's ways and are specifically designed to influence us to sin so that he can bring defeat and failure into our lives.

Temptation is based on a lie. In essence, it is a form of false advertising. The devil tempts us by advertising something illicit and gives false promises about the results it will produce. He promises us, just as he did Adam and Eve, that our sin will bring no adverse consequences. The end result of sin, however, always will be exactly what God's Word says it is: "The wages of sin is death" (Rom. 6:23).

Just think about what Satan told Eve when he convinced her to go ahead and eat the forbidden fruit. He said to her, "You will not surely die" (Gen. 3:4). Eve bought the lie and—they did surely die. They first died spiritually, and ultimately they died physically. That was not God's plan for them. Had they not eaten that fruit, Adam and Eve never would have died. They would have gone on living forever in the beautiful creation God had designed for them.

The fact is, sin opens the door to deception. Deception opens the door to more sin—which inevitably results in further defeat and failure. That is why it is so important for us to walk in truth. We must rely on the information God has given us, not on what the devil says. When we act on God's information about sex (which is the truth), we are not going to be ashamed. When we get married, we'll enjoy sex in marriage the way God intended, and our sex lives will be beautiful, fulfilling and a blessing.

But when we act on information about sex from the devil (which is deception), shame and defeat will poison our lives. The fruit of deception will cause us to do the same thing Adam and Eve did: We will begin to hide from God, live in shame and fear, and be unfulfilled in our sexuality.

Never forget that the door to deception is opened in our lives through sin.

Remember how as soon as Adam and Eve sinned, the devil began waging his campaign of subtle lies to bring them into bondage. He said, "There's something wrong with you, with your sexuality. You need to hide from God, because He's ashamed of it. If you allow Him to see it, He will judge you for it." Of course, God had not changed His mind about Adam and Eve, or His plans and purposes for their lives. But Satan had succeeded in changing the way Adam and Eve thought about their sexual relationship.

As a result of the enemy's deception, rather than running to God and confessing their sin, this couple was quaking in fear, hiding from God and from one another. And so God's beautiful gift of sex was destroyed.

satan's "sex ed 101"

The devil certainly didn't make deception about sex and sexuality his primary target without thinking it through carefully. I believe he targeted this area of our lives because he realized sexuality could be used as a handle to control us. Our sexuality is an integral part of who we are, and if he can control our sexuality, he can get a grip on a fundamental part of our identity.

As long as we walk this earth, we will be sexual beings. It doesn't matter what our station in life—single, married, young or old—sex will always be a part of who we are. So we must understand God's design for that part of our nature and learn to walk in His ways.

It is true there are rare people who are able to live their lives without expressing their sexuality. These people have received the gift of celibacy. People in the Bible who were celibate were by no means a "subculture"; rather, they were a "superculture." As single people, they had been *given* the *gift* of celibacy in order to be free to serve God in a superior way. The apostle Paul spoke about the fact that he had the gift of celibacy. Further, he wished that everyone could be celibate so that they could be free to serve God without the distractions of sex (see 1 Cor. 7:7).

If you are one of those people who are called to celibacy, you know it is a special gift from God.

Most of us, however, have not received—and are not meant to have—the gift of celibacy. Paul says that those who don't have that gift should marry (see 1 Cor. 7:1-5). In other words, it is best for the vast majority of us to fulfill God's plans for our sexuality within the marriage covenant, as He designed. God created us as sexual beings, and we remain sexual beings our entire lives.

As we've discovered, God had a glorious plan in mind when He created sexuality. It was for one man and one woman to live together in a lifelong, covenanted sexual relationship. We've also clearly seen that from the beginning, the devil devised a plan to attack sexuality and use it for his evil purposes.

Remember, Satan is a strategist. He conspired to attack us at the core of our existence. He determined to pervert the Creator's intention for sexuality. He schemed to take sexuality out of the light of the Garden and into his realm of darkness. He understands that once he gains control of our sexuality, he has the ability to control other facets of our lives as well. At the very epicenter of the devil's vicious plot to pervert our God-given sexuality, we find *deception* as his strategy.

Satan's Strategy of Deception

This tactic will always be a part of Satan's method of operation because deception is part of his very nature. Jesus made clear to us that Satan is the father, or originator, of lies and deception: "There is no truth in him. When he speaks a lie, he speaks from his own resources, for he is a liar and the father of it" (John 8:44).

Lies are Satan's "resources" and a huge part of his strategy. Eve found that out firsthand. When the serpent came to her in the Garden, what did he do? He lied to her. He distorted the truth of what God had said. Listen to how he caused her to question the truth, how he tried to persuade her to believe something God didn't say. He cleverly posed a question designed to introduce doubt into her mind: "Has God indeed said, 'You shall not eat of every tree of the garden'?" (Gen. 3:1).

God had not said anything of the sort! The truth was, God had commanded the man and woman to freely eat the fruit of every tree in the Garden—except one.

> The LORD God planted a garden eastward in Eden, and there He put the man whom He had formed. And out of the ground the LORD God made every tree grow that is pleasant to the sight and good for food. The tree of life was also in the midst of the garden, and the tree of the knowledge of good and evil. Then the LORD God took the man and put him in the garden of Eden to tend and keep it. And the LORD God commanded the man, saying, "Of every tree of the garden you may freely eat; but of the tree of the knowledge of good and evil you shall not eat, for in the day that you eat of it you shall surely die" (Gen. 2:8–9,16–18).

Eve's response reveals she knew the truth—at least in part:

> And the woman said to the serpent, "We may eat the fruit of the trees of the garden; but of the fruit of the tree which is in the midst of the garden, God has said, 'You shall not eat it, nor shall you touch it, lest you die'" (3:2–3).

At first, Eve didn't *fully* buy the lie—but, at the same time, she didn't have the truth *firmly* planted in her heart either. So, the serpent pressed for the advantage. He didn't give up, but rather *again* he lied and cultivated the seed of doubt he had just planted: "You will not surely die. For God knows that in the day you eat of it your eyes will be opened, and you will be like God, knowing good and evil" (Gen. 3:4–5).

This lie was intended to make Eve believe that God was withholding something good from her. By implying that God's words weren't really true and by calling into question God's goodness and character, the serpent successfully deceived Eve into disobeying God's instructions. As you know, the results were catastrophic.

Eve sinned. She believed and acted on Satan's lies. She ate of the tree of the knowledge of good and evil, and death entered the world—just as God had said. No longer would humankind enjoy the gift of immortality.

The Serpent's Brand of Sex Education

The serpent was no fool. He had won the initial round, so he pressed hard for the next victory. The fact that Adam and Eve had believed his first lie gave him a foothold in their lives. With a vengeance, he then attacked their glorious gift of sexuality.

This time, his lies and deception devastated them with shame. Adam and Eve, for the first time, became ashamed of their sexuality. They sewed fig leaves to cover themselves. Instead of being open and honest, they began to hide from God and from each other.

But it didn't end there. Shame was the beginning. Disharmony between the spouses soon followed. The sexual act no longer signified the oneness God had meant for husband and wife to enjoy. Yet sin, especially sexual sin, is like that—it leads to destruction. Believing one lie and stepping into sin opens the door to more deception and more devastation.

Satan gained entrance into the human psyche through deception. He began to whisper to Adam and Eve that their sexuality was dirty and shameful. He cast a shadow on sex itself, brought it under his control, and he began to instruct Adam and Eve with his lies.

When this happened, the devil became the default sex educator of humankind. And from the beginning, that was the real intent of his conspiracy. He wanted couples to be ashamed to express their needs and desires so that they would be frustrated and tempted to seek satisfaction outside their marriage. He wanted parents to be ashamed of sex so that they wouldn't teach their children God's plan for them as sexual beings—leaving him free to lure them into sexual sin. He wanted biblical truth about human sexuality to be mocked as outdated and meaningless. And he has been successful, deceiving minds and hearts through an aggressive marketing campaign—on the Internet, in theaters and on your television.

Using temptation, deception and his own evil brand of sex education, the enemy has been able to corrupt and control entire cultures. We don't have to look far to see the evidence of his "education" all around us. In our society, the devil's lies run rampant. His view of human sexuality is honored as the authority, while biblical truths on the subject are scorned. These lies are creating unspeakable heartache, destruction and confusion in the hearts and minds of people everywhere.

This is all part of the devil's strategy to control us and thwart the purposes of God in the earth. His goal is to twist our sexuality, weaken the covenant of marriage and destroy our relationship with the Father. God, however, is the true sex educator. He created us, and He created sex as a gift to us. He wants us to enjoy our sexuality within the marriage covenant, and thereby fulfill His purposes in the earth. In order to do that, we must recognize what the serpent's lies are, and shine the light of God's truth on them. We must, like Paul, imitate the mission of Jesus Himself. He reminds us that He came "to open their eyes, in order to turn them from darkness to light, and from the power of Satan to God, that they may receive forgiveness of sins and an inheritance among those who are sanctified by faith in Me" (Acts 26:18).

Do you need God's light in your life? Has the devil successfully convinced you of his version of the truth—which is deception? Has that deception led to sin? If so, don't lose heart. As we continue to shine God's truth on the lies of the enemy, you will find the power of darkness losing its grip on your life. Knowing the truth will help you be free. It will bring you into your amazing inheritance in the kingdom of God.

Let's take that beacon now and focus it on some lies that Satan likes to use in an effort to control our lives.

PART II

the conspiracy
spreads:
12 common lies
about sex

CHAPTER 4

lies #1 and #2:
redefining sex and love

Lie #1: It Is Not Really "Having Sex" Unless You Have Intercourse

Ever heard this one before? "You are not really having sex, unless you are having intercourse." Parents, you need to know that the enemy chants this lie to our young people. He's endeavoring to subtly change their thinking by redefining sex and love.

In fact, this thinking has become very prevalent among high school and college-age students in our society. Those who have accepted this lie are convinced there is nothing wrong with engaging in sexual activities as long as they don't involve intercourse. Many people—teenagers especially—think petting, masturbation or engaging in oral sex is acceptable because it is not really "having sex." Some experts believe this mindset became prevalent when former president Bill Clinton was accused of sexual misconduct. I'm sure you remember that incident!

When pressed about his sexual relationship with a White House intern, Clinton stated that he "did not have sex with that woman" because they did not have sexual intercourse. It seems his statement had an impact on the younger generation, because this philosophy has now become popular in our culture. So, parents, talk to your children about what the Bible says! Talk to them about what Jesus has to say about the subject: "But I say to you that whoever looks at a woman to lust for her has already committed adultery with her in his heart" (Matt. 5:28).

He makes it clear that sexual sin occurs even when there is no physical contact. Indeed, sexual sin can occur in the heart. In God's sight, even looking at someone else with the thought of committing a sexual act is the same as physically committing that act.

Please understand that Jesus is not talking about times when you might have a fleeting thought about sex. Anyone can be tempted for a moment. If you are a living, breathing human being, then at one time or another, you have had a sexual thought. What you choose to do with that thought will make it sin—or not.

When a tempting sexual thought comes to your mind, you have several options. Think of it as if it were a game show and the host (God) is offering you a prize that is behind one of three doors.

The right "door" to choose would be Door #1—otherwise known as "casting down imaginations." Second Corinthians 10:5 (*KJV*) says that when thoughts that go against God's Word come to your mind, you need to be "casting down imaginations, and every high thing that exalts itself against the knowledge of God, and bringing into captivity every thought to the obedience of Christ." Just as you are instructed to "resist the devil and he will flee," soo too you are instructed to resist impure thoughts, and they too will flee from you.

There are, however, other choices.

Behind Door #2 is the choice called "entertaining that thought." When you choose this door, you give over your imagination to the thought, expound upon it and continue to think about it. If you begin to fantasize about having sex, undressing a person in your mind, then the thought becomes sin. If you walk through this door, you walk smack into the arms of *lust*. Even if you have no physical contact with that person, Jesus says that you have already committed the act of sexual sin—you have sinned by looking on a person with lust.

Of course, there is Door #3, also known as "acting on that thought." Walking through this door means physically engaging in sexual sin.

And, as I said, regardless of what Bill Clinton or anyone else thinks, the Bible says sexual sin includes things other than intercourse.

The idea that sex is not really sex unless there is intercourse is one of the serpent's more insidious lies. Fallen humankind is always looking for ways to justify sin, but we shouldn't forget that God is always looking on the heart. God says that it is possible to commit sexual sin in the heart.

Sexual intercourse and any other kind of sexual touching are reserved for marriage only. Anything outside of that is sin. It is important to teach this truth to our children because they are constantly being bombarded with the serpent's lies. "Sexual *touching* is not really sex" is his message. "Oral sex is not really sex." The bottom line is that touching a person sexually or being touched sexually is "sex"—and sex is to be reserved for the covenant of marriage. Why? Because our bodies are temples of the Holy Spirit and are designed to reflect God's plan for our human sexuality.

> Do you not know that your body is the temple of the Holy Spirit who is in you, whom you have from God, and you are not your own? For you were bought at a price; therefore glorify God in your body and in your spirit, which are God's (1 Cor. 6:19–20).

In the Old Testament, the temple of God was the temple that Solomon built in Jerusalem; in the New Testament, God's temple is our body. Since we know that things in the Old Covenant are really a type and a shadow of the good things to come in the New Covenant (see Heb. 8:5; 10:1), if we look at the pattern for the Temple described in the Old Testament, we can understand more about God's design for our "temples."

In the Old Testament, the temple of God had four courts: the outer court, the inner court, the Holy Place and the Holy of Holies.

The outer court was open to just about anyone: Men and women of all ages, even Gentiles, were allowed into the outer court. Because this area was open to the general public, it was called "the Court of the Gentiles."

The inner court was the second part of the Temple—and access to it was restricted. This area was open to the air but divided by a high curtain. Only the priests, the sons of Aaron, could enter the inner court.

The next area was covered, and no one could see into it. A highly restricted area, it housed both the Holy Place and the Holy of Holies. When a priest stepped into this covered part of the Temple, he first stepped into the Holy Place, which held the lamp stand, the table of showbread and the altar of incense. The Holy Place was a very special place, and only a few of the priests were allowed to enter into it.

Beyond the Holy Place was the Holy of Holies, where the Ark of the Covenant was kept. Only one person was allowed to go into the Holy of Holies, the High Priest, and he was only allowed to enter in on one certain day of the year.

Let's look at the correlations between the Temple of God in the Old Covenant and the present-day temples of God, which are our bodies. Just as Solomon's Temple had four courts—four levels of intimacy with the Lord—so too our bodies can be considered to have four "courts," or areas, of physical intimacy.

For example, the "outer court" of my body would be the area that is open to just about anyone, such as my hands or my forearm. A total stranger could approach me, and I would reach out and shake hands. He could even grab my forearm, and that would be all right. Just about anyone could touch the "outer court" of my body. But I would not want a total stranger to touch me beyond those "outer court" areas.

The "inner court" of my body is a bit more restricted. Those areas are only accessible to someone I'm close to, such as a friend or a relative. If I have a close relationship with someone, he might hug me, pat me on the back or even touch my face. But I would not want just anyone to be that familiar with me. Those "inner court" areas are reserved for people I know well—people with whom I have a relationship.

Then there are the "Holy Place" areas of my body. Only a select few people can touch me in those areas. For instance, only in certain situations would my doctor, my mama and my wife be able to touch my bottom or my lips. No one else has access to those "Holy Place" areas.

Finally, the "Holy of Holies" on my body would be my genitals. Only *my wife* is allowed in this very private place. No one else.

The same should be true for all of us. Only our spouse should be allowed to touch us in a sexual way. Our bodies are temples of the Holy Spirit—they do not belong to us, but to God. The sexual parts of our bodies are our Holy of Holies—they are to be touched by only one person: the person we are married to.

Lie #2: It Is Not Wrong to Have Sex with Someone You Really Love

Many people have fallen for this lie. They say, "Well, I know it is wrong to have sex with someone you barely know. I would never have casual sex. I only have sex with someone I really love. And if we really love each other, what could be wrong with that? Sex is the best way to express our love."

Remember when you were a teenager and your hormones were raging? You experienced a lot of emotions, but those feelings were not really love. Those feelings were infatuation—nothing more than "puppy love," which can be here today and gone tomorrow.

We need to know and teach our children that true love is based on the love of God. True love is a sacrificial love that is willing to commit to a person for a lifetime.

"True love" is genuine love when there is a commitment behind it.

In trying to justify sex outside of marriage, some people may even say, "But we really are committed to one another. God understands our hearts, and we are already married in God's sight." That is a lie. There is only one way to be married in God's sight, and that is to get a preacher and gather your family, and stand up before witnesses to make vows to be committed to and love each other forever. You cannot pronounce yourself married in the back seat of a car!

Many young men are guilty of trying to use this line to convince a girlfriend that it is okay to have sex. Young girls can also be guilty of the same offense, but I believe it is more common for young men to try to persuade girls to yield to their desire for sex. I was a very immoral young man before I gave my life to the Lord. I am not proud of that fact—it is one of the greatest regrets of my life. But let me just be honest and say that I—and a lot of my friends—said "I love you" just so a girl would go along with what we wanted to do. Unfortunately, some of those girls believed us.

I confess this in order to make parents aware, and hopefully help young girls be forewarned, that the "I love you, so sex is okay" line is commonly used by young men. A guy may put tremendous pressure on his girlfriend to have sex, but that young lady needs to know the truth about his motive. And the truth is—it's not true love. It's lust.

So, parents, tell your young girls this:

A boy may say that he loves you, but until he is standing in front of a preacher and he has put a ring on your finger, and relatives and friends are sitting there (watching him like a hawk), and he commits the rest of his life to you in the presence of God—it is not true love.

A lot of fancy words and empty promises are the hallmarks of deception. So in anticipation of the day when a boy will pressure your daughter by saying, "If you love me, then you will let me," teach your daughter not to hesitate to tell him, "If you love me, you will not put me in that position! If you love me, you will not threaten to abandon me if I do not have sex with you."

Love does not take. Love gives.

Love does not demand something in a selfish way. Love commits and sacrifices.

A Risk of a Lifetime

There is another ugly truth about the serpent's brand of "love" that he tries hard to hide. He doesn't want anyone to think about the consequences of engaging in sex outside of marriage. But the truth is: sin has devastating consequences. Sexual sin in particular carries grave risks: sexually transmitted diseases and the possibility of pregnancy.

Young people between the ages of 13 and 24 years old need to realize the cold hard facts that they are the most susceptible to sexually transmitted diseases because their bodies have the greatest vascular blood flow. To date, there are 20 known sexually transmitted diseases (STDs). Once upon a time, a shot of penicillin could cure many of these diseases, but now a lot of STDs are drug resistant, and no effective treatment exists. Other sexually transmitted diseases, such as herpes or AIDS, have always been incurable.

Many STDs are asymptomatic, which means there are no symptoms for a time. Infected people can have a disease—and pass it on to others—without knowing it. Examples of asymptomatic STDs include the human papilloma virus and chlamydia. Chlamydia is the most commonly transmitted sexual disease in America today. It can be passed from person to person with neither the male nor the female having any knowledge of infection. They only find out much later when symptoms begin to manifest. Many people believe condoms will protect them from diseases like this, but condoms are of no use against chlamydia—and most other STDs.

Girls who have sex at an early age are the most vulnerable to these sexually transmitted diseases and, as a result, often suffer from cervical cancer and other major reproductive problems later in life. Chlamydia can be devastating to a woman's health. Not only is it a major cause of cervical cancer, but it can also cause infertility.

Girls need to understand the tremendous risk involved in having sex with a boy just because he says, "I love you." They need to be aware of the possibility that that guy could be sharing a disease with them—and that disease could affect them for the rest of their lives.

Would love really ask someone to take that risk?

Sex outside of marriage also makes people vulnerable to the AIDS virus. In America, this disease is most prevalent among homosexuals. However, in other regions of the world, AIDS is just as common in heterosexual relationships as in homosexual relationships. It, too, can be asymptomatic for years. Someone can be infected with the virus without knowing that he or she has this incurable disease.

And of course young people should never forget that promiscuity brings with it the risk of pregnancy. A young man may say he loves a girl, get her pregnant and then abandon her to raise the child alone. It happens every day. What assurance does a girl have that a guy will really stick by her if she should become pregnant? None.

In the same way, an unwanted pregnancy can be devastating to a young man's life. Sad to say, there are some girls who get pregnant deliberately in an attempt to keep a young man tied to the relationship. Parenting responsibilities would be thrust upon him long before he is prepared for it. So young men need to be aware that they are not immune from the consequences of sexual sin by any means.

Obviously sexual sin is *not* God's plan. Sex outside of marriage is not God's idea of "love." God's idea of love is for a man and a woman to commit to each other and to Him in marriage *before* they have sex.

What Is True Love?

The words "I love you" are nothing but words until that love is demonstrated by commitment in marriage. God's love always thinks about what is best for the other person. This is what God says about love: "'You shall love your neighbor as yourself.' Love does no harm to a neighbor; therefore love is the fulfillment of the law" (Rom. 13:9-10).

What would happen in the dating arena if this were the theme?

If you have a teenager, ask him or her to give this some thought. Point out that chances are good that the person your son or daughter is dating now is not the person he or she will marry. And chances are just as good that your teen's future spouse is dating someone else right now. Put it to them this way: *Right now you are dating someone else's future spouse. And someone else is dating your future spouse. How do you want your future spouse to be treated?*

The truth is, often guys have a double standard about dating and sex—they want the women whom they marry to be untouched and pure. However, they don't feel the necessity to remain pure. They want to have sex with other women before marriage.

But a guy should consider the fact that his future spouse is probably dating someone else right now. Does he want her to be honored and treated with respect? Or does he want her to be pressured into having sex? Does he want to marry someone who has a disease or who has someone else's baby?

Jesus said, "And just as you want men to do to you, you also do to them likewise" (Luke 6:31). If a man wants his future wife to be treated respectfully, he should treat the girls he dates likewise.

The Bible makes it clear that the things we do today will come back to us tomorrow: "Do not be deceived, God is not mocked; for whatever a man sows, that he will also reap" (Gal. 6:7). We cannot expect to reap a good harvest in a future relationship if we are sowing seeds of disrespect and selfishness right now. The best way to ensure that our future spouse is treated with honor and respect is to honor the people we date. The Bible talks about this quite plainly in 1 Thessalonians:

For this is the will of God, your sanctification: that you should abstain from sexual immorality; that each of you should know how to possess his own vessel in sanctification and honor, not in passion of lust, like the Gentiles who do not know God; that no one should take advantage of and defraud his brother in this matter, because the Lord is the avenger of all such (4:3-6).

God does not call sexual immorality "love." He says sexual immorality is *defrauding* and *taking advantage* of someone. He also makes it clear He will avenge those who have been wronged in this way—which in itself is a very good reason to keep the true love of God in mind during all dating relationships. The love of God will never lead us to take advantage of someone else. Rather, it is characterized by commitment and sacrifice. The love of God will inspire us to save sex for marriage—which is where it belongs.

In the Fig Leaf Conspiracy, the devil sells "love" as just a feeling, and insists that "love" inspires selfish sexual behavior. The "love" that demands sex outside of marriage is not love at all. It is just another deception from the serpent.

lies #3 and #4:
test drive before you buy

Lie #3: The More Sexually Experienced a Person Is Before Marriage, the Better Lover That Person Will Be When Married

The serpent wants people to believe that sexual experiences before marriage will make them better lovers. But exactly the opposite is true. I have found that people who have the most satisfying sexual relationship in marriage are those who have had the least sexual experience before marriage. In reality, heartache and a fear of true intimacy are the hallmark of sex before marriage. Damage from previous relationships makes it more difficult for a person to open up emotionally when he or she does get married.

Why is this a problem in the bedroom? Because *emotional intimacy* is what makes a sexual relationship most fulfilling—and sex before marriage attempts to take the place of true communication and intimacy. Rather than enhancing the relationship, premarital sex is a hindrance to developing the relationship skills needed for true intimacy.

Beyond presenting a barrier to emotional intimacy, premarital sex often results in sexually transmitted diseases—a point we covered earlier. But in the context, consider that a single person who has been sexually active with multiple partners for five years or more has a 100 percent chance of contracting a sexually transmitted disease, and then bringing that disease into his or her marriage. As you know, many of these diseases are incurable.

Exposing your spouse to an STD is hardly sexy. Neither is contracting something incurable from him or her. Considering that, how could anyone believe that having sex outside of marriage will make a person a better lover?

Contrary to Satan's lies, sex before marriage has no positive benefit. Instead, it brings heartache, a sense of abandonment and disease. The truth is that the happiest people are those who have followed God's plan and saved sex for marriage. The best lovers are not those who have learned about sex from sin—the best lovers are those who have learned about sex from God, and from one another.

Lie #4: Sex Before Marriage Deepens Intimacy and Helps Couples Know if They Were Really Meant for Each Other

Satan peddles the lie that sex equals intimacy. That simply is not true. Sex can be an *expression of intimacy* that already exists. Sex can be an *expression of love* that is present between two people. But sex cannot *create* intimacy or love. And when sex is used as a substitute for true intimacy—or as a counterfeit for love—it is a hindrance, not a help.

In our culture, we often use the term "making love" to describe "having sex." This is quite a deception! Having sex with someone does not "make" love occur. Laying down your life for someone "makes" love. Sacrificing for someone else and building friendship through selflessness "makes" love. But sexual relations cannot *create* or *make* love or intimacy.

True intimacy is the result of emotional closeness, respect and honesty. True intimacy arises out of trust and genuine friendship. Having sex before marriage does nothing to foster these vital components in a relationship. Instead, sex before marriage creates relational laziness and disrespect—attitudes that are fatal to true intimacy and love. Yet the devil is doing a good job of convincing people that cohabitation—having sexual relations and living together before marriage—will help their relationship. Fifty percent of all people who are getting married today have lived together prior to saying "I do."

But, not only does God's Word clearly tell us that sex before marriage is wrong—statistics also prove it is counterproductive. More abuse exists in cohabitation than in marriage. And a couple that has lived together before marriage has a 70 percent chance of divorcing. Clearly, when sex becomes the focus in a relationship, building a strong foundation of trust and friendship is neglected—and the marriage ends up resting on sand, not rock.

So, why do people do it? Typically, a woman agrees to live with a man because she believes that it will strengthen their relationship. She is hoping that living together will take their relationship to the next level—marriage. A man, on the other hand, tends to live with a woman before marriage so that he can enjoy the benefit of sex without the responsibility of marriage. But the motivation of both the man and the woman prove that choosing to live together before marriage is a decision based on selfishness, not love.

Covenant marriage, on the other hand, is based on the love of God. Covenant is selfless, not selfish. In a covenant relationship, a person gives away his or her "rights" and assumes "responsibilities." The spirit of covenant says, "This is all about you, not about me. I am committed to you, for better or worse, for richer for poorer, in sickness and in health, to love and to cherish, till death do us part. Regardless of circumstances, I will serve you and cherish you for the rest of my life. I will take care of you and love you no matter how hard things may be. I am committed to you, and to this marriage, forever."

How extraordinarily different is the spirit of cohabitation! Cohabitation is, in effect, a contract—not a covenant. And it's a contract that easily can be broken. The spirit of cohabitation says, "This is all about me and what I want. I am going to see how good you are at taking care of me before I make a commitment to you. If you measure up, then I might marry you. But if you do not meet my needs, I will leave you."

Cohabitation is not based on true love—it is based on performance. It is like being on stage constantly. If you do not measure up, the relationship is over.

True love mirrors the love of God—and it operates very differently. Hebrews 13:5 gives us insight into His love and how marriage should function: "I will never leave you nor forsake you" is God's idea of covenant love. He accepts us with all of our faults and weaknesses. He calls us His children even when we don't deserve it. There are times God could justify leaving and forsaking us, but He never does.

Jesus paid the price for our sins and weaknesses, and we are always accepted and forgiven and loved by the Lord. That is Good News! I am so glad that God's loving kindness toward us is not dependent on our performance. On our worst days, God is still our very best friend.

> Who shall separate us from the love of Christ? . . . For I am persuaded that neither death nor life, nor angels nor principalities nor powers, nor things present nor things to come, nor height nor depth, nor any other created thing, shall be able to separate us from the love God which is in Christ Jesus our Lord (Rom. 8:35,38-39).

That is the love of God. He gave His only Son to die for us so that we could become His sons and daughters. He is committed to us forever. That is the love of a covenant relationship. That is the kind of love that makes a marriage successful.

While dating, a couple should be learning how to communicate with each other, solve problems together, and enjoy time together as friends and companions. If they are not having sex, a couple will be free to develop the core of their relationship. Then the qualities of true friendship—communication, trust and respect—are allowed to blossom. These are essential to true intimacy. But if sex comes into the picture before marriage, it tends to become the primary focus and distracts from building that foundation (this is particularly true for men because they are not as relational as women).

A man will lose a lot of motivation to work on the relationship once he begins having sex with his girlfriend. If a problem arises in the relationship, he may want to solve it by having sex. If he is bored, having sex will fix that. If there is a disagreement, he may want to have sex, rather than work to resolve the issues that created the conflict in the first place.

If sex is his answer to everything before he is married, it will be his answer for everything after he is married. He won't make the effort to be romantic. He won't feel the need to talk. When there are problems, he won't put forth the effort to work on the relationship. He will be a lazy husband because he already expects to get something for nothing.

The truth is, if a woman has sex with a man before marriage, he will lose respect for her, and true love will never blossom without respect.

Saving sex for marriage enables true friendship to develop and lays the groundwork for a successful marriage. It forces the man to treat the woman he will marry with respect. It forces him to learn how to communicate, to solve problems and to work through anger. It forces him to fill times of boredom with romance and conversation, and to build true intimacy. It forces him to pay the price to establish a friendship—he must "wine and dine" the woman he professes to love and demonstrate that he is willing to work on the relationship in nonsexual ways.

Sex is very precious to God, and it ought to be precious to us. It should never be shared outside the covenant of marriage. And it should never be used as a substitute for the love and intimacy that come from true friendship.

The purpose of dating is not to find out how good someone is in bed. The purpose of dating is to determine the character of the other person; to see how spiritually compatible two people are; to start building the foundations of friendship and trust that make a marriage last a lifetime. Yet the serpent tries hard to convince people they need to find out what kind of lover their significant other is before they commit to marriage. Of course, nothing could be farther from the truth!

"Intimacy" means "inner closeness," and it is that inner closeness that makes sex truly fulfilling. The greatest intimacy between two people exists when both have a vital relationship with the Lord Jesus Christ. When two people know God and are intimate with Him, they have a wonderful foundation on which to build a relationship in marriage far beyond anything the world has to offer. When a foundation of communication, trust and commitment is there, so is intimacy—which means sex can be phenomenal. But sex can never be a substitute for that foundation.

CHAPTER 6

lies #5, #6 and #7:
remove the limits and enjoy the thrill

Lie #5: The Restrictions God Established for Sex Are Puritanical and Keep People from Enjoying Sex to Its Fullest

The devil wants us to believe that God doesn't want us to experience any pleasure, let alone great sex. He tries to make people believe that God's Word is outdated and His laws exist just to ruin the fun. Naturally that isn't true.

As we take a look at the restrictions God has established for sex and talk about His reason for giving us those restrictions—it becomes crystal clear that God established those boundaries for our benefit. The "do nots" actually make up a pretty short list and they can be summed up as follows:

- No sex outside of marriage (adultery *and* fornication)
- No homosexuality (same-sex relationships)
- No bestiality (sex with animals)
- No pornography
- No fantasy lust (looking at another person with intent)
- No pedophilia (sex with children)
- No incest (sex with family members)

I imagine most people agree with the majority of this list.

Yet the serpent still is on a campaign to make us think God is *denying* us pleasure when He forbids these things. The kinds of sexual activity outlined above, however, will lead only to pain and despair. The reason God has placed sexual boundaries in our lives is to us keep from destroying ourselves and others.

The Bible is the instruction book God has given us to tell us how to live our lives successfully. We could think of His Word as an owner's manual for humanity. It's much like the manual I have in the glove compartment of my car—that manual contains detailed information about my car's make and model. It gives very exact instructions about what to do and what not to do. It gives specific directions about how to maintain that car and keep it in good working order.

Of course, the manual also features yellow warning emblems to make me aware of what can damage the car. When I read my car's owner's manual, I don't get offended when I see a warning sign. I don't say, "The people who wrote this are just a bunch of fuddy-duddies who are trying to control my life." I do not accuse the manufacturer of trying to keep me from having fun and enjoying my car. No. If the manual says to put 30 pounds of air in the tires, I do not put in 15 pounds. I assume their advice is meant to help me keep my car in good working order—they designed it, so they know best.

Because I like my car, I take care of it according to the manufacturer's instructions. I don't want my car breaking down—I want it to run smoothly and efficiently, the way it was designed to run. So I take the advice given in the owner's manual.

In the same way, the Word of God is the owner's manual for our lives. It was given to us by the God who created us, and He is not a killjoy who is trying to keep us from enjoying sex. He is a loving Father, and He created sex as a beautiful gift for us to enjoy. His "owner's manual" lets us know how to experience true fulfillment in our lives. He doesn't want us to miss out on any of the blessings He has designed for us. Nor does He want us to participate in sexual activities that will rob us of those blessings. He knows what will bring us joy and fulfillment, and what will lead to death and destruction. So, in effect, He has placed big yellow warning signs next to the dangerous activities He knows will destroy us and our happiness.

Modern research is now proving what God has known all along: All the "forbidden" sexual activities are extremely harmful and can destroy a person's life, health and happiness.

But the serpent has been very successful in distracting people from the scientific realities. He instead focuses on appealing to our rebellious human nature, portraying these forbidden sins as pleasurable "musts." He attempts to convince people they are missing out on something if they adhere to God's standards for sexuality. The truth is, the only thing they will miss out on is heartache and pain. Proverbs 14:12 tells us, "There is a way that seems right to a man, but its end is the way of death." While the serpent works hard to make these sins that lead to death "seem right"—apart from the redemption of Christ—adultery, pornography, homosexuality, pedophilia, incest and bestiality will destroy a person's life. These sins will lead to misery and bondage rather than genuine fulfillment and happiness. You do not have to look very far in our society to see the pain and suffering caused by these behaviors.

A Lifetime of Delight Is Available

There is a lifetime of delight for those who will follow God's plans and obey His laws. There are so many ways for a husband and wife to enjoy the gift of sexuality. And if a married couple will submit this area of their lives to God, He will continually refresh and bless their relationship.

In the Song of Solomon, we are given a picture of the love between Christ and us, and also a beautiful picture of a sexual relationship between a husband and wife. In the seventh chapter, these lovers are talking about the different ways they can enjoy their relationship with each other. They say:

There I will give you my love. The mandrakes give off a fragrance, and at our gates are pleasant fruits, all manner, new and old, which I have laid up for you, my beloved (vv. 12–13).

There are all kinds of "pleasant fruits," or pleasures, the married lovers have saved up for one another. They have saved their sexuality to be shared in marriage. There is no need for a husband or wife to look anywhere else.

Further, God has promised a continuous supply of "pleasant fruits, all manner, new and old" for a loving couple—in other words, He will continue to make the sexual experience between a married couple exciting and new. We find in chapter one, verse 16, these telling words: "Also our bed is green." That Hebrew word, "green," means "verdant" or "flourishing," like a healthy plant that is always growing new leaves and producing new flowers. That is the sort of sexual relationship God has promised to us! If we will follow His "owner's manual" and yield this area of our lives to Him, He will see to it that sex is always exciting and fresh—bringing new life into our marriage relationship.

Once while teaching this topic, I made the rhetorical statement, "There are millions of ways to enjoy sex within marriage." Afterward, a man came up to me and said, "Name them, will you?" I don't think his curiosity was healthy. True, God designed sex within marriage to be a constant source of discovery and delight, but an unnatural lust or perversity that arises out of selfishness and greed is not what God intends.

The love of God has a supernatural ability to bring life to anything and everything, including the gift of sexuality. God has promised us that marriage always can be refreshed by His love and vitality if we live within the parameters He has set.

If we don't stay within His guidelines, however, we open ourselves up to the enemy, and certain trouble. Jesus tells us, "The thief does not come except to steal, and to kill, and to destroy. I have come that they may have life, and that they may have it more abundantly" (John 10:10). That's pretty plain. Jesus came so that we could have life more abundantly—that includes "abundant life" in the area of sexuality. He came so that we could be free from all the sorrows that come with sin, including sexual sin. If we believe and follow His Word, we will experience joy and peace in our sexual relationship. We will be blessed.

If we don't obey His Word, however, we will be headed for destruction. Given half a chance, the devil will steal the joy of our sexual relationship. He will kill the love between a husband and a wife, and destroy the beauty of God's creation by drawing God's man and woman away from His design for sex, and into perversion and sin.

Remember what the serpent said to Eve: "Has God indeed said . . . You will not surely die, for God knows that in the day you eat of it your eyes will be opened, and you will be like God" (Gen. 3:1,4–5). Nothing's changed. The serpent wanted Eve to believe that what God had said was a lie—but it was the serpent that lied. The serpent said they would not die if they disobeyed God's commands—but they did die. He said that they would be like God if they disobeyed God's commands—but they did not become like God. They became more like the devil: selfish, fearful and ashamed.

The serpent has no new tactics. He is still lying to us. He is still trying to deceive us. He wants us to believe sexual sin will not end in destruction. But it does.

Lie #6: The Most Fulfilling and Exciting Sex Is Outside of Marriage for Those People Who Are Not Encumbered by Biblical Morality

This idea is another attempt to discredit God's "owner's manual." The serpent says that the true pleasures of sex cannot be experienced within the confines of marriage. He wants people to believe that the best sex is "out there" somewhere in a fantasy world of "swinging singles."

This idea gets a ton of press! And the media seems intent on promoting this mindset.

At one time, *Playboy* magazine was the chief promoter of pornography. Now, however, there are countless magazines, websites, movies and television shows that portray immorality as "the norm"—or as harmless fun and games.

Take *Sex in the City*—a show that is now broadcast on network television. It features a group of glamorous and very promiscuous young, single women who "cat around" and have sex with every person who strikes their interest. *Desperate Housewives* is yet another program that endorses sexual immorality and promotes the idea that sex outside of marriage is an exciting and acceptable lifestyle. Such "entertainment" erroneously teaches that there is more pleasure and fulfillment in sexual immorality than in marriage.

The serpent just licks his lips and claps his hands in glee at this kind of programming! As people watch these shows, he has a grand opportunity to tempt them to sin. "You know your marriage is really boring and monotonous," he whispers. "Really great sex is to be had by people who aren't encumbered by the archaic shackles of biblical morality. Give it a try. No one will ever know."

Unfortunately, even some Christians are being deceived by this lie! Influenced to believe sex is better outside of marriage, married believers are being drawn into a lifestyle of sin. I know married women who have ventured into the bar scene, saying, "Well, I married at a young age, and I missed out on what life really has to offer." They become deceived into thinking that the free-and-easy lifestyle portrayed on shows such as *Sex and the City* is real. They begin looking for some mythical "soul mate." More than one woman has abandoned her husband and family to go looking for the *illusion* of the perfect man and a more exciting lifestyle, only to find a world of heartache—which is always what the serpent's lies bring.

No married person should look over the fence at the glamorous girls on *Sex and the City* and lament about all the fun he or she is supposedly missing. Those actresses who pretend to live promiscuous lives are *acting*. The lives they portray as so glamorous and exciting are *illusions*. These actresses do not live a *Sex and the City* lifestyle in everyday life.

People living a lifestyle of sin do not "have it all." They are experiencing hurt and devastation. They are struggling with emotional trauma—and feelings of emptiness and worthlessness.

The truth is that the greatest sex is within marriage! I once read a study that concluded that married people have sex more often than single people and are also more satisfied with their sex lives. Another study revealed that the most sexual and orgasmic women in America are those who are married, monogamous, deeply religious and Protestant!

Those in the secular world may have been shocked by these findings, especially if they had swallowed the serpent's lies and believed that swinging singles have the best sex. But if you believe the Word of God, you won't need a scientific study to tell you that married sex is the most satisfying. You'll know that when you are tuning in to what God has to say about sex, rather than listening to what the serpent has to say about it, the smile on your spouse's face tells the whole story!

Of course, there are also some very practical reasons why married sex is better than the "swinging single" life.

First, a husband and wife do not have to fear contracting a sexually transmitted disease, and sex naturally thrives in an atmosphere that is free of fear and insecurity. Having sex outside of marriage means taking a huge risk—and fear can inhibit sexual freedom and expression. Faithful married couples don't have that fear hanging over them like a cloud. They can fully enjoy sex because they are safe in a covenant that binds them to one another.

A second reason sex is better within marriage is that marriage creates an atmosphere of trust and security. Promiscuous sex occurs "in the moment" and is based on feelings that come and go. The relationship may be here today and gone tomorrow, so there is little or no trust between partners—and no sense of security. Doubt and insecurity do nothing to make sex meaningful or satisfying.

In marriage, however, a husband and wife are committed to each other for the long haul. They are not concerned about their partner seeing their flaws or leaving them during tough times. They can feel safe in the relationship and can experience trust that makes sex more fulfilling.

Can sex be more exciting and fulfilling outside of marriage, like the serpent says? Absolutely not. The best sex is always in an atmosphere of emotional closeness, security, trust and commitment. God designed marriage as that place of commitment where safe, exciting and satisfying sex can take place.

Lie #7: The Bible's Sexual Standards Are Unfair to Homosexuals, Transsexuals and People Who Are Born a Certain Way

Sexual sin is widely accepted in our society. God's Word is often viewed as terribly unfair to certain groups of people, including homosexuals. The serpent tries to cast doubt on God's goodness and love. By creating confusion and doubt about God's nature, the devil has had a measure of success in convincing people that God's standards for sexuality are unfair.

But, the truth is, God is *incapable* of being unfair.

The serpent has always tried to convince people that God is unjust and withholds good. Remember, that was his tactic in the Garden of Eden with Adam and Eve. He tried to smear God's character and made Him out to be the bad guy.

But God simply is not capable of being unfair, because He is not capable of being *wrong*. The Bible tells us, "The judgments of the Lord are true and righteous altogether" (Ps. 19:9). God's decisions are always right and true. His commandments are fair and just. He is incapable of giving an unfair, unloving commandment, because God *is* love.

If we have a problem with something He has commanded, the problem is in us and in our thinking, not in Him or His Word. If God says we should not do something, it is for our own benefit that we steer clear of that "something."

As Christians, we have trusted in Christ and we have a relationship with Him through the Cross. If we truly trust in Christ, then we will trust in His Word to us. We will trust in His goodness and His love. We will trust that God's commandments regarding sexuality are fair.

Here is what He says about the subject:

Do you not know that the unrighteous will not inherit the kingdom of God? Do not be deceived. Neither fornicators, nor idolaters, nor adulterers, nor homosexuals, nor sodomites, nor thieves, nor covetous, nor drunkards, nor revilers, nor extortioners will inherit the kingdom of God (1 Cor. 6:9–10).

Certain sins can prevent us from inheriting the kingdom of God. And, contrary to what the serpent says, God is not unfair about this judgment at all. Notice, He does not say that one sin is worse than another; He does not make a distinction between adultery and homosexuality, or between being a fornicator and being a thief. He says that people who *practice* these sins are not going to inherit His kingdom: "Let no one deceive you with empty words, for because of these things the wrath of God comes upon the sons of disobedience" (Eph. 5:6).

Before you begin to tremble over the sins you know you have committed, let me just emphasize that there is a difference between *committing* a sin in a moment of weakness and *practicing* sin as a lifestyle. When God says that the unrighteous will not inherit the kingdom of God, He is talking about those who willingly and knowingly turn their back on God's laws and deliberately choose sin as a lifestyle.

When we make Jesus our Lord and are born again, we become new creatures, and our sins are washed away. We are not "the unrighteous" any longer, but are "made the righteousness of God in Christ." If we sin, as all of us do, "He is faithful and just to forgive us our sins, and to cleanse us from all unrighteousness" (1 John 1:9).

Before I accepted Christ, I was an "unrighteous" person and, had I died, I would not have inherited the kingdom of God. I practiced sin as a lifestyle, and I had no intention of changing. When I welcomed Jesus into my life, I repented of those sins, and the Lord forgave me and made me a new creature in Him. I am no longer classed with "the unrighteous"—through the blood of Jesus, I have been "made the righteousness of God."

Of course, I endeavor to live my life as pleasing to God, but sometimes I still fail. When I do, I go to God immediately and repent of my sin. This is not the same thing as *practicing* sin.

Someone who is *practicing* sin has no intention of stopping—and in fact pursues his sinful lifestyle with a passion. A *practicing* homosexual is not someone who is struggling with homosexual feelings and resisting them. A practicing homosexual says, "I choose this sin for my life, and I have no intention of turning away from it."

A *practicing* adulterer is not someone who had a one-night stand during a moment of weakness. A practicing adulterer is someone who carries on a long-term affair—and he has no intention of turning away from that illicit relationship. By way of illustration, let me tell you a specific situation that occurred during one of my marriage seminars.

After one service, a couple approached me. The husband proceeded to tell me that he had a mistress and had no intention of giving up that relationship. In front of his wife, he began justifying this behavior to me. When I told him that what he was doing was wrong in the eyes of God and that he had to turn away from that sin, he refused. In spite of what the Bible said and what I said, and in spite of his wife's misery, he made it plain he had no intention of ending his adulterous affair.

This man was not *committing* a sin—he was *practicing* sin. This kind of behavior is what God is talking about when He says, "the unrighteous will not inherit the kingdom of God." In God's eyes, as a *practicing adulterer*, that man was in the exact same category as a *practicing homosexual*.

People deal with tendencies toward sin because we all have a sin nature. God lets us know we must resist every tendency to sin. He is not unfair about it. In spite of what is politically correct in our culture, homosexual behavior is not exempt from what God's Word says about it. God has commanded us to refrain from *all* sexual sin.

The serpent tries to sell the lie that homosexuality is a special kind of sin because "Homosexuals are born that way. They can't help it." The truth is, every one of us is born in sin, and every one of us is born with the tendency to sin. No one had to teach us to be immoral and sinful. It comes naturally to us!

For instance, though I was not born with a tendency toward homosexuality, I definitely was born with a tendency toward sexual immorality. As a young man, I immediately yielded to those tendencies. I did not have to learn how to sin. After I surrendered my life to God, I had to learn how to resist those lustful tendencies and bring those temptations to Him.

We all deal with some tendency toward sin. Some of us may deal with a tendency toward homosexuality while others deal with a tendency toward covetousness. God knows our weaknesses. He is not shocked when we are tempted to sin, and He does not make a distinction that one sin is worse than another. But He does make it clear that we must resist our sinful tendencies. It is up to us to resist—and we can. He would not command us to do something He hasn't given us the ability to do.

No temptation has overtaken you except such as is common to man; but God is faithful, who will not allow you to be tempted beyond what you are able, but with the temptation will also make the way of escape, that you may be able to bear it (1 Cor. 10:13).

God has made "a way of escape" from temptation—that way is Jesus! He gave His only Son to die for us so that we could be free from the bondage of every sin. He will not condemn us when we are tempted; but He commands us to stay away from sin because He knows it will destroy us. Through Jesus Christ we can overcome every temptation, and God expects us to do just that.

The God who created everything is not going to change what He said about sexual sin in order to be "politically correct." When people say that homosexuals and transsexuals are just "born that way," they are saying there is something intrinsically wrong in the way God created people. Not true. God never created anyone to be homosexual or transsexual. *What sort of God would create someone to be a certain way and then forbid that person to be that way?* Not the loving God in whom we have put our faith and trust.

We have been made in the image of God. If there is something ungodly in our nature, it comes from sin. Sin was not part of God's creation; sin came through man's rebellion against God's Word. It is true that we are born with a tendency to sin; that tendency is a result of the Fall.

No one has to teach a room full of toddlers how to be selfish. They have been born with the tendency to take that toy away from the child next to them! But God did not give them that evil tendency. It came through the sin Adam and Eve brought into the human race when they listened to Satan's lies and disobeyed God's word.

If convicted thieves told us that they just couldn't help stealing—if they said, "When I walk through a store, things just stick to me"—

would we buy their line? Would we excuse their behavior because they may have been born with the tendency to steal? No. We would recognize that they have a responsibility to control the urge to steal.

God did not create anyone to be a thief, nor did He create anyone to be a homosexual, a transvestite or a transsexual. Before going any further, let me clarify the meaning of these terms:

A *homosexual* is a person who keeps his or her own sexual identity to some degree but who chooses a same-sex partner. A *transvestite* is a person who is confused about his or her sexual identity and dresses as a person of the opposite sex to try to deal with that confusion. A *transsexual* is a person who has had surgery to alter his or her sexual parts. Transsexuals surgically change their bodies to be like that of the opposite sex. Transsexuals claim to be either "a man trapped in a woman's body" or "a woman trapped in a man's body."

People who are involved in practicing these sins are definitely confused about their sexual identity. Political correctness says that they have been intrinsically created that way; therefore, it would be cruel to forbid them from discovering and living out their "true identity." That is the deception of the serpent. The devil conspires to confuse and torment people about who they really are. He hates God's creation and endeavors to rob people of their God-given identity and purpose.

When God created humankind, He made everything to function correctly, with a purpose, according to His design. God looked at everything He had created and declared it was very good. And He created us. The Bible tells us He knit each one of us together in our mother's womb:

> For You formed my inward parts; You covered me in my mother's womb. I will praise You, for I am fearfully and wonderfully made; marvelous are Your works, and that my soul knows very well. My frame was not hidden from You, when I was made in secret, and skillfully wrought (Ps. 139:13-15).

We are fearfully and wonderfully made, formed skillfully by the Master—He knew exactly what He was doing when He created us. The serpent, however, says God makes mistakes—sometimes. That is a lie. When God is forming someone in the womb, He does not say, "Oops, there I go again, putting a woman in a man's body! Too bad—I guess they'll just have to be miserable." No, God created each one of us with a wonderful purpose in mind, and our sexuality is part of that purpose. God did not create a man to lust for another man or a woman to lust for another woman. And God did not create anyone as a man who is really supposed to be a woman.

If we want to look for the real origin of homosexuality and gender confusion, we need look no further than the devil himself. The devil is very cruel, and he hates human beings. He delights in bringing them pain. And so I do not judge those who have been harmed by him in this way. On the contrary, my heart breaks for them.

Many people suffer tremendously during childhood when sexually or physically abused, or when severely neglected. Such suffering and pain in children can create serious wounds. The devil uses these hurts as inroads into people's lives. He starts whispering lies to them about their identity. He says things like, "God doesn't love you! He made a mistake when He made you. You are really a woman trapped in a man's body." Or he says, "You can never feel attracted to the opposite sex; you can only be attracted to your own sex." This lie of gender confusion is simply part of the serpent's conspiracy to destroy people and God's purposes for their lives.

Of course, the devil's scheming isn't limited to those who suffer with gender confusion and same-sex attraction. As I've said, I didn't struggle about my sexual identity as a young man, but I certainly did struggle with immorality. I couldn't seem to help myself when it came to sexual sin, even though I had grown up in church. It might shock you to know that I would spend Saturday night sinning and then show up to sing in the choir Sunday morning. I had no guilt whatsoever! When I was a young man, the force of sin was driving me, and it seemed I was powerless to stop it.

When I finally became disgusted enough with my own behavior, I got down on my knees, repented of my sins and asked God to forgive me. I asked Jesus to come into my life and change me. And He did! He made me a new creature. He delivered me from sin and gave me the power to overcome those sins I had been powerless to overcome on my own. For over 30 years now, my life has been dramatically different because of His grace, His love and His power.

Without Jesus, none of us has the power to overcome sin. He lived a sinless life. And He defeated sin on the cross for us. He took on our sins and shed His blood as a sacrifice for those sins. He made the way for us to come into right relationship with God. His power is much greater than the power of any sin. His grace is always able to see us through any temptation. When we call upon His mercy, He helps us in our weakness. He gives us the ability to overcome what we could never overcome on our own.

God did not create sin, and He is not responsible for the fact that it exists. He has delivered us from sin by sending His only, perfect Son to die for us. He has made a way for us to live in peace and freedom and victory. But it's up to us. If we refuse His grace and continue practicing sin, God says we will not inherit His kingdom.

The serpent says the Bible creates prejudice against homosexuals. But the truth is that the Bible calls homosexual behavior sinful just as it says adultery and fornication are sinful.

People create prejudice, not God and not His Word.

God is not against people—He is against sin. Jesus died for every person. He bore every sin.

God is neither prejudiced nor hypocritical. The Bible tells us He "is no respecter of persons." His love extends to every person, and His

Word is true for every person—equally. As His children, we are supposed to be like Him. We are supposed to love every person the way He loves every person. However, that doesn't mean we are to condone their sin, because we know sin results in destruction.

The serpent desperately tries to convince society that rejecting homosexuality is a form of prejudice. He desires for us to go along with this lie so that he can destroy people by convincing them they were "created" as homosexuals. People who are caught in this ugly snare of homosexuality need us to help them escape. We do that by telling them the truth. As Christians, we must tell them about The Way of escape from sin. We are commanded to share with others how they can experience newness of life in Jesus Christ.

Those who are in bondage to homosexuality or any other sin don't need to feel the pain of hatred or bigotry. They need to hear the truth: God loves them and has a better way for them to live. It is the goodness of God that leads men and women to repentance. God's mercy and loving-kindness are what draw people to Him.

When I was in the depths of sin, I was drawn toward God by a young lady who was very pure morally, and she treated me better than I deserved. She did not condone my sinful behavior, but she did not reject or condemn me either. Her demonstration of God's unmerited love drew me to Christ and changed my life forever.

Through Jesus Christ and the power of the cross, I have been able to live in victory in the area of sexuality. But I know I could still stumble. As a human being, I am not immune to temptation. I must walk humbly before God every day, trusting Him to help me live uprightly before Him.

That's true for all of us. And the serpent knows it. He knows we are weak and struggle with temptation. *That's why another facet of his treachery is to cry "hypocrite" if we dare stand up for biblical standards.*

Jesus dealt with this issue when the Pharisees brought an adulterous woman to Him. They made sure to remind Him that the Law said she should be stoned. The Bible tells us they were trying to trap Jesus so they could accuse Him. If Jesus had said she shouldn't be stoned, He would have been disagreeing with the Law. On the other hand, if Jesus had said she should be stoned, they would have accused Him of being judgmental and not showing mercy. Jesus avoided their trap by pointing their attention to something much more important: "He who is without sin among you, let him throw a stone at her first" (John 8:7).

Jesus didn't disagree with what the Law had said about sin. He didn't condone adultery or try to excuse the woman's behavior. But neither did Jesus condemn her. Instead, He directed attention away from that woman, instead inviting the onlookers to examine their own hearts.

Jesus was reminding us that there is not one sinless person among us. It is not our place to judge others and condemn them. As Christians, we have been forgiven and set free from sin. It is our place to love others and to share with them the truth that set us free. That is what Jesus did:

When Jesus had raised Himself up and saw no one but the woman, He said to her, "Woman, where are those accusers of yours? Has no one condemned you?" She said, "No one, Lord." And Jesus said to her, "Neither do I condemn you; go and sin no more" (John 8:10–11).

Jesus is our example. He does not want us to condone sin, because sin brings destruction. He wants us to hold up the light of His truth and be witnesses of His redemption, His ways and His plans. We should no more condemn people than God condemns us. We are to love them just as He loves us and set us free from sin.

God wants us to tell people about His goodness, His mercy and His love. He wants us to let the world know that in Jesus there is the power to "go and sin no more."

CHAPTER 7

lies #8 and #9:

women have the gift and power of sex

Lie #8: A "Normal" Man Should Be More in Touch Emotionally—There Is Something Wrong with a Husband Who Wants Sex All the Time

One of the saddest consequences of the Fig Leaf Conspiracy is the way the devil causes men and women to reject—rather than rejoice in—one another's unique differences. It is a fact that God created men and women to have very different sexual needs and drives. The serpent tries to use those differences to drive men and women apart, and to create division rather than love.

When a man and woman get married and sex becomes a part of their life together, there is a tendency for the woman to reject her husband's sexuality. Many times a wife will believe there is something wrong with her husband if he has a strong sex drive. She may think her husband is perverted because his need for sex is greater than hers.

That's natural, however. Men have a greater desire for sex than women because *God created men that way.* Male sexuality is a powerful force. You can accept that fact or reject it, but there is nothing you can do to change it—because God is not going to change what He designed (which was all good, if you recall).

Women, on the other hand, tend to have a greater need for communication than do men. God designed men and women with these differences *deliberately* so that they will learn from one another and serve one another.

If a man wants his wife to be happy, he is going to have to be much more communicative than is natural for him. He must realize that his wife has a greater need for deeper, more intimate communication than he does. If a husband talks to his wife only as much as seems normal to him, his wife is not going to be satisfied.

In the same way, if a woman is only sexual when she feels like it, her husband is going to be very miserable and frustrated sexually.

A survey was taken in which men and women were asked about the importance of sex in their lives. The results were not at all surprising. Men replied that sex was among the top three things that they absolutely could not live without. But when women were asked how important sex was to them, it ranked twelfth or thirteenth (along with things like gardening).

This does not mean women are completely nonsexual. It simply indicates that women are not as naturally inclined toward sex as men are, and thoughts about sex don't occupy much of their time. An understanding and loving husband, however, can help his wife become more in touch with her sexuality—and more of a source of pleasure and relaxation for her. After all, sex is to be used to love and serve one another, not just to gratify self.

Another difference between men and women is the way they are sexually stimulated. Women are turned on by a man's character. This is supported by the results of another survey in which women were asked, "When do you find your husband the most sexually attractive?" The number one answer women gave to that question was "When he is doing housework."

Some men have a hard time believing that! Because men are visually stimulated, they tend to think the way to get a wife interested in sex is to spend time at the gym, get a tan and walk around with their shirt open. A man's wife, however, is most likely to walk by and lovingly pinch him when he is doing the dishes.

It's easy to see how problems arise in marriage, specifically in the area of sex, when a husband and wife fail to understand and accept the differences between men and women.

Today, our old friend, the devil, is promoting a lack of understanding regarding these differences. In particular, the serpent is promoting the lie that men ought to be like women when it comes to sex. "If only you had married a 'normal' man," he whispers, "he would not want sex all the time. A normal husband would understand how you feel about sex, and he would feel the same way you do about it. Instead, *you* are married to a *sex maniac!*"

And women are listening to these whisperings. The average wife these days assumes that having more sex with her husband would only "feed the monster." She may say something like, "You want sex way too much, buddy. You must be thinking dirty thoughts if you are interested in sex *all* the time. Besides, only some sort of sex fiend could ever be attracted to this body of mine."

Which brings us to another issue, courtesy of demonic influence: Many women are inclined to have low self-esteem. Women are pushed by society to measure up to an external standard of "perfection" that makes them constantly aware of any real and imagined flaws. The devil will use a woman's low self-esteem to attack the intimacy between a married couple. When a woman is convinced her body is unattractive, she will not understand how her husband could be sexually attracted to her—she believes that her husband's interest in *her* sexually just proves he is some sort of sex monster.

A "normal" husband, however, will be stimulated by the sight of his wife's body. And a "normal" husband will want to have a lot more sex (and a lot less communication) than his wife. Yet here again the devil is working mischief, by seeking to convince women that a good husband would talk more and want less sex. The sly one uses romance novels and soap operas (what I call "women's entertainment") to promote this way of thinking. The hero typically is a "sexy" looking, very emotional man who is more interested in communication and feelings than he is in sex. Soap-opera relationships are brimming over with romance. The men depicted in these stories, however, are nothing like real men. Most men are not content to always hang around and be romantic and talk about their feelings. Though laughable in a way, this sort of "entertainment" is also damaging. It strips men of their God-given uniqueness. The men in unrealistic tales have been desexualized and made to seem extremely emotional and romantic—every woman's "dream guy." Yet for women to entertain this kind of fantasy is actually not so different from men indulging in pornography. Soap operas and romance novels do to men the same thing pornography does to women: *degrades. Objectifies. Creates a standard that is not only impossible, but also unnatural.*

Women don't tend to think of romance novels and soap operas as being very sexual because the focus is more on the emotions of the relationship than the sexual part of it. But in reality, these stories are all about lust and fantasy—and some of these stories are very obscene as well. In the end, they portray men as something other than what they really are, and create an unrealistic illusion. Instead of helping women understand men, these "stories" feed a fantasy that leads to dissatisfaction and disharmony.

Let me illustrate: A husband drives off for work, and while he is gone, his wife spends time at home reading her "Sir Hunk-a-Lot" book or watching "As the Stomach Turns" and filling her head with unrealistic images of men. Just as she has finished wiping the tears from her eyes after watching another emotional episode between "Lance" and "Melissa," her husband "Stan" walks in the door. Unlike "Lance" (who is always mysteriously well groomed and gentlemanly), Stan looks rather tired and doesn't smell that great. And then, as if to add insult to injury, Stan grabs her and kisses her—without ever asking her how she's feeling!

And then what happens?

Such indignation! Such emotional outrage and tears! *To think how Lance and Melissa have such a beautiful relationship, how they talk to each other about their deepest feelings and wildest dreams—yet I am married to a Neanderthal Man who thinks of nothing but sex!*

Can you understand how this kind of "entertainment" is responsible for a lot of misunderstanding and misery? The TV world is a fantasy world that feeds human selfishness—it does nothing to inspire true intimacy. It gives women the idea that the perfect "soul mate" would be more interested in emotions and feelings than in sex. But that simply is not the way men are created. A real man will want sex much more than he wants communication and emotions.

A woman who accepts her husband understands that God created him with a greater need for sex. She realizes sex is not something that must be endured in a marriage but rather sex is a beautiful gift God created with purpose. She knows it is the most normal thing in the world for her husband to want to have sex with her. *God has created that need in the man so that he will "cling to his wife" and keep coming back to her.* Sex is a gift God has given to the woman so that she might serve her husband and bring fulfillment to his life.

Likewise, a man needs to understand that God created his wife with a greater need for emotions and communication, and he needs to do all he can to meet her needs in those areas.

When a couple is no longer prey to these deceptions, they have figured out the conspiracy—and are no longer under the devil's destructive influence. Once they understand and accept one another for who they really are and who God created them to be, they are well on their way to enjoying true intimacy.

Lie #9: Sex Is a Powerful Weapon Women Have to Control Men and Get What They Want from Them

God has given men the need for sex—and given women the gift of sex. God's plan is for a husband and wife to serve one another with sex, within the covenant of marriage. Yet the devil wants to take what God has created, twist it and use sex as a control mechanism.

One of the ways he does that is by convincing women to use sex as a "weapon." When a woman goes along with the devil's scheme, the marriage relationship is tremendously harmed. Why? Because God created sex as a gift to *serve*. Not as a tool to *control*.

Many females realize at a very young age how powerfully men are affected by sex. They quickly discover how to use sex appeal to attract men and get what they want from them. Many women develop a pattern of using sex as a way to control men, and then that behavior carries over into marriage. This type of selfish behavior is devastating to the relationship, since a marriage is a covenant based on *giving*—not *getting*.

The Bible describes a covenant relationship between a husband and wife in 1 Corinthians:

> Let the husband render to his wife the affection due her, and likewise also the wife to her husband. The wife does not have authority over her own body, but the husband does. And likewise the husband does not have authority over his own body, but the wife does. Do not deprive one another except with consent for a time, that you may give yourselves to fasting and prayer; and come together again so that Satan does not tempt you because of your lack of self control (7:3-5).

This Scripture tells us we lose authority over our own bodies when we marry. If a wife wants to have sex, her husband has no right to deny her, because his body is no longer his own. If a husband wants to have sex, his wife has no right to deny him, because her body is no longer her own. If a wife withholds sex or tries to use sex to manipulate her husband, she is violating the covenant of marriage. In the covenant of marriage, each person gives up his or her own rights and accepts responsibility for the other.

This does not mean that a husband or wife has the right to abuse or to make a spouse participate in unscriptural or sinful acts. Our bodies also belong to God:

> Or do you not know that your body is the temple of the Holy Spirit who is in you, whom you have from God, and you are not your own? For you were bought at a price; therefore glorify God in your body and in your spirit, which are God's (1 Cor. 6:19–20).

What does this mean? It means we have no right to use our bodies for our own selfish purposes. Our sexuality is a gift from God, and He gave us that gift so that we could serve one another, not control one another. We have no right to use His gift of sexuality as a tool to control or manipulate our spouse.

Sex is the covenant sign of marriage, and God takes it very seriously when His covenant sign is used in the wrong way. For this reason, it is a dangerous thing for a woman to use sex to control a man. It transforms the spirit of the woman, and it also changes the spirit of the marriage, opening the door to the operation of an evil spirit often referred to as a "Jezebel spirit." This demonic spirit works to control and manipulate men through the use of sex (we read about the operation of this spirit in both the Old and New Testaments).

In the Old Testament, Jezebel was the evil wife of Ahab, one of the wicked kings of Israel. She persecuted the prophets of God and promoted the worship of idols. Jezebel would make herself beautiful in order to control the men around her, especially her weak-willed husband, Ahab, who allowed himself to be manipulated by his wife. He also ran to her for answers when there was a problem. His behavior only made that controlling spirit stronger.

The same dynamic occurs today. When a woman is controlling, the man is weak; and when the man is weak, it encourages the woman to become more controlling. The two always go hand in hand.

In the book of Revelation, the Lord Jesus Christ comes to the church at Thyatira and rebukes them because they have allowed this spirit to operate in their midst.

Nevertheless I have a few things against you, because you allow that woman Jezebel, who calls herself a prophetess, to teach and seduce My servants to commit sexual immorality and to eat things sacrificed to idols. And I gave her time to repent of her sexual immorality, and she did not repent. Indeed I will cast her into a sickbed, and those who commit adultery with her into great tribulation, unless they repent of their deeds. I will kill her children with death, and all the churches shall know that I am He who searches the minds and hearts (Rev. 2:20-23).

The leaders of this church allowed a woman named Jezebel to manipulate them with sexual immorality and to seduce them into teaching idolatry. The Lord Jesus Christ says He will cast her and all those who go along with her wicked schemes into a sickbed. Then He says something that should make every one of us stop and think. Jesus says, "I am He who searches the minds and hearts."

God knows what is going on. He knows what is inside each person's heart and mind. If a man is allowing a woman to control him through the use of sex, God knows about that. If a woman is using sex to control and manipulate a man, God sees that. If there is no repentance, He will not allow that sin to go unpunished.

Notice that Jesus does not speak to the woman Jezebel in this passage of Scripture. Jesus speaks directly to *the male church leaders* who are *allowing* this woman to manipulate and control. He is holding these men responsible for the sin and idolatry she is bringing into the church. From this we learn that when a woman uses sex to control and manipulate a man, the man is held to greater accountability because a woman can only control and manipulate him if he is weak.

Jesus said that He had "something against" the male leaders of that church, and He put it in these words: "You *allow* that woman Jezebel . . ." Jesus made it clear that men should not allow themselves to be controlled or manipulated in this way.

When a wife uses sex to control her husband, the marriage will be devastated. Why? A man wants and needs to be loved, not used and controlled. He wants his wife to have sex with him because she loves and cares about him. A wife shouldn't insist upon having everything going her way before she is willing to have sex with her husband. If she does—and makes a habit of controlling the relationship through sex— her husband eventually will become resentful of her manipulation. And, if he continues to allow her to manipulate him, the Bible makes it clear he will be held responsible for not doing something about it.

A man must not permit a controlling spirit to take root in his life and family by allowing his wife to manipulate. Not only will he be affected, but a weak man also sets that example for his children *and* robs his wife of the kind of husband she really needs. A wife needs a husband who is willing to be a leader—a man who will stand up for what is right.

When a husband refuses to take responsibility for his marriage, he will soon see how that controlling spirit will bring destruction to his family *and* invite the judgment of God. If a man refuses to stand up to a Jezebel spirit, the devil will rob him and his wife of the true joy God has planned not only for their sexual relationship, but also for their very lives, family and ministry.

This Jezebel spirit is seeking to control more than just our families. It is seeking to control our entire society. Media and marketing campaigns are using the sex appeal of women to sell everything from music and movies to food in a restaurant. Scantily and seductively dressed celebrities are often using sexual appeal in place of talent to manipulate people into buying their particular brand of "stardom." This is nothing more than a Jezebel spirit at work.

Of course, it is unwise to allow a Jezebel spirit to control our decision regarding how to spend our money. As Christians, we need to realize much more is at stake than an isolated transaction—say, buying a pair of jeans. If a business is using sex to try to solicit business, I go elsewhere. I'm interested in knowing about the product being offered, not in the seductive image of a woman's body. If I allow such an image to influence my spending, I am permitting a Jezebel spirit to gain ground in my life and the culture as a whole.

It seems this Jezebel spirit has infiltrated every aspect of our society. Men are affected by it, women are affected by it, and, sadly, many young people—girls in particular—are being affected by it. Bombarded with the message that sex appeal is everything, young girls—who often struggle with low self-esteem—are focusing on conforming to that image rather than on living out God's purpose for their lives. The devil attempts to draw these young women into his snare by suggesting that sex appeal is the way to gain acceptance from their peers, and attention or admiration from boys. So, many innocent girls begin emulating the actresses and musicians they admire.

Our job as parents is to keep a close eye on the development and behavior of our children. Teaching them the Word of God, training them in godly behavior, making sure they have healthy friends and helping them build strong self-esteem through the love and acceptance of their family are vital in protecting them from a controlling Jezebel spirit. If we do not protect our children, they will certainly fall prey to the mischief wrought by this spirit.

My now happily married daughter is very beautiful, and when she was growing up, it was my job to protect her. And, believe me, it was a big job, since a lot of boys were interested in her. One way I protected her was to make sure she was dressed appropriately before she left the house. I was not a prude. I was simply helping her understand that she didn't need to use sexual beauty to get attention. We taught her that if a girl has to use her body to attract a boy, something is very wrong. The wrong spirit is behind that kind of thinking. Sexuality is a precious gift from God, and it is never to be flaunted to gain attention or to manipulate others.

If, from a young age, a girl uses her body to influence the men in her life, a Jezebel spirit gains a foothold. Before long, this destructive spirit will wreak havoc in her life, and follow her into marriage. The result? Usually devastating for the young woman's family. When a woman uses her sexuality to control her husband, it has an emasculating effect on the man. It hurts the children and causes the family to be dysfunctional. More serious problems begin to develop when such a woman loses her sexual appeal. After all, no one stays young forever. What happens when that young, sexy, attractive body changes as the result of sickness, pregnancy or just the natural process of aging? Well, that controlling spirit will not give up simply because a woman isn't as beautiful as she once was. When the Jezebel spirit can no longer use seduction and manipulation to get its way, it turns to something even worse: intimidation and domination.

There are two prongs to a Jezebel spirit: seduction and intimidation. Some women tend more toward the use of seduction, and some more toward the use of intimidation. Using seduction or intimidation to control is a grievous sin in the eyes of the Lord. Remember, anyone who misuses sexuality in this way pays a severe penalty. Jesus says, "Indeed I will cast her into a sickbed, and those who commit adultery with her into great tribulation, unless they repent of their deeds. I will kill her children with death" (Rev. 2:22-23).

Because this woman has used sexuality to seduce His servants, Jesus says He is going to cast her on a sickbed, along with the men who allowed her to control them this way. In other words, she is going to suffer in her physical body. That sexual appeal she has used as a means of control and manipulation is going to wither away. Then judgment will come, both on her *and* on the men who allowed her to control them. The destruction also will have a devastating effect on her children.

Never is this God's will. He created women with sexual beauty as part of His great plan and purpose for sex. His intention is for women to use that power of attraction as a gift to serve their husbands and fulfill His plans for sexuality. Yet because of the Fall, women seek to manipulate men—they struggle with a desire to influence their husbands in particular: "Your desire shall be for your husband, and he shall rule over you" (Gen. 3:16).

In God's order of authority, the man is the head of the woman. In this passage of Scripture, we discover that women will struggle to some degree with their husband's God-given authority. It is only natural for a woman to want to influence her husband. But because of the curse that God spoke in the Garden, the devil will always be tempting her to fulfill that desire using sinful means.

Contrary to God's design, the serpent attempts to get women to use sex to control and manipulate their husbands. The Bible spells out the order God has established:

Wives, likewise, be submissive to your own husbands, that even if some do not obey the word, they, without a word, may be won by the conduct of their wives, when they observe your chaste conduct accompanied by fear. Do not let your adornment be merely outward—arranging the hair, wearing gold, or putting on fine apparel—rather let it be the hidden person of the heart, with the incorruptible beauty of a gentle and quiet spirit, which is very precious in the sight of God (1 Pet. 3:1–4).

A woman is not to use her outward beauty or sexual appeal to "win" her husband. Instead, a wife should win her husband by her chaste conduct and the hidden beauty that is in her heart. The word "chaste" means "pure, clean and modest." A godly woman does not need to flaunt her sexuality to win her husband. Neither does she need to use lots of words—or intimidation. Her conduct will speak for itself and show her husband what is hidden inside her heart. Her "gentle and quiet spirit" will speak volumes to her husband and be pleasing to the Lord.

The serpent says that women should use sex to control and manipulate men. But God says a woman influences her husband by the way she lives her life: by loving him, by praying for him, by serving him. And by being an example of the love of God.

The love of God never uses the gift of sex as a tool to control or manipulate. The love of God always uses the gift of sex to serve.

lies #10, #11 and #12:
sexual sin doesn't really hurt anyone

Lie #10: "Normal" Women Are Not Emotional or Complicated and Should Be Very Sexual, Just Like Men

Pornography is a huge problem in our culture today. One of the most damaging things it does is give men a false idea about women. Since men are naturally very sexual and visually oriented, they would like to think their wives are the same way. The serpent wants men to believe women are just like men, and he uses pornography to create the deceptive illusion.

Pornography portrays women as very sexual and non-emotional. The women who are pictured in pornography do not need to talk about their feelings. They do not need to feel connected to the man with whom they are having sex. They are not preoccupied with the kids or worried about getting the grocery shopping done. The women in these pictures are focused on one thing—they just want to have sex.

Pornography is a picture of the way some men wish women would be. In many ways, pornography is an illustration of how men approach sex, but it has very little to do with the way women really feel about sex. If you are married, this probably doesn't surprise you. In the same way women's entertainment (romance novels and soap operas) portrays men as having the psyche of a woman, pornography portrays women as having the psyche and sexuality of a man.

Of course, this is not reality, but for many men who view pornography, the damage has already been done. Studies show that being exposed to R-rated, sexually explicit material as few as five times fundamentally changes the way a man views women. By portraying women as very sexual and non-emotional, this material encourages a man to objectify them and see women primarily as sex objects. Once a man has swallowed this lie, the devil can hinder him from understanding a woman's real needs, which will result in his never experiencing true sexual fulfillment in marriage.

A husband must learn to understand his wife's true needs before he can experience the joy God intended for their sexual relationship.

Women are *complicated*. Women are *emotional*. A woman can wear out a mood ring in five minutes! If you think she is in a bad mood, just wait a few minutes. If you think things are all rosy and happy, just wait a few minutes more. A husband must understand the way his wife is created and learn how to relate to her.

When it comes to sex, men are very "compartmental," while their wives are "inclusive" about it—in other words, a woman's feeling about sex is affected by everything else that is going on in her life. A man is definitely not that way. Consider this, a man may have the worst day he has ever had at work, followed by the news that "Armageddon is tomorrow"—and he will still be interested in having sex. A man's attitude tends to be, "Well, since everything else is falling apart, we might as well have sex. After all, what better way to spend our last few moments on Earth?"

Women are the opposite way. Sex for a woman is tied together with all the other issues of her life—the children, the neighbors, the washing machine that's broken and the tree that is dying in the backyard. All of those things affect her emotions, so all of those things affect her sexuality.

The serpent does not want men to understand this dynamic about women. The serpent says to men, "The children? The washing machine? The tree that is dying? What is wrong with her? Is she crazy?!"

There is nothing wrong with her, and no, she is not crazy.

God made her to be very complex and emotional, and He wants her husband to understand that about her. God expects her husband to love her, listen to her and help her through all the concerns in life—and to do so in a sensitive and understanding way.

If a man looks at pornography and sees women who do not seem to be emotional or complicated, he may believe this lie the serpent is selling about women. He starts thinking to himself, *These women are "good to go." They are interested only in making your sexual fantasy come true. They don't need to be cared for or nurtured. Those women do not cry. They are not complicated, like my wife. She wants to talk, share about the kids and pray for her mother's broken finger. I don't want to bother with all that. I just want to have sex. I'm going to go find a low-maintenance woman.* Caught in a web of deception, many husbands then abandon their families and go in search of that imaginary woman.

If a man left his wife and actually married a Playboy bunny, she might pretend to be a sex goddess for a while. But it would not be long before the man discovered that she is no different from any other woman. If she is a woman, she will be emotional and complicated, because that is the way that God created her to be. She will need nurturing and love and communication, just like every other woman. Before long he discovers that she is just as "high maintenance" as the wife he left behind!

Women are not as sexually inclined as men. A loving man, however, can help a woman become much more sexual. But he can never do this by treating her like a sex object. He does this by caring about her needs. He does this by being sensitive to her concerns and feelings.

The way for a man to stir up his wife's sexual desire is to communicate with her. Listen to her aspirations, hurts, fears and concerns. She needs him to serve her and help her navigate through day-to-day problems. When a man comes home from work and says, "Honey, go take a bubble bath and let me take care of the kids for a while. I'll wash these dishes and vacuum the floor. And don't fret about your mother. I am going to call her right now and pray for her broken finger." That wife will take her bath, put on a pink teddy and before he is finished with the dishes, she'll be calling from the bedroom, "Honey, come in here."

Women are emotional. Women are complicated. And women are meant to be cherished. When a man objectifies a woman and sees her as a sex object, he is missing out. He is not seeing who she really is—a unique human being, who needs her husband's love and understanding, and who has so much love and affection to give in return.

Why did God create this dynamic of opposites in marriage? I believe He wants men to have to work at His greatest gift, which is sacrificial love. He wants to help men learn to be servant-leaders, as Jesus is. And I also believe that God wants to ensure that selfish men do not get the best sex! While no woman should withhold sex from her husband just because he is insensitive or selfish, an insensitive and selfish man will miss out on something wondrous. He will miss out on helping his wife discover the full potential of her sexuality.

And that is exactly the serpent's intention: He wants to destroy the beauty of what sex can be when a husband and wife understand and serve one another the way God intended.

A man who understands the way God created women will begin to understand his wife. As he becomes a servant to his wife, loving and cherishing her, he will see her sexuality blossom like a rose.

Lie #11: Pornography and Other Sexual Sins Can Spice Up One's Sex Life and Make It Better

The thinking of many men—even Christian men—has been so shaped by pornography that they actually believe introducing sin into their marriage will actually spice up their sex life. I am not proud to admit that I myself was like this when I was first married. The devil had been my sex educator, and he had me convinced that looking at racy movies and pornographic material would make our sex life more exciting. Of course, my wife, Karen, would have nothing to do with this. Her response frustrated me. Listening to the serpent's lies about sex had caused me to be very deceived.

And I am not the only one who has fallen prey to his lies. Many men have had the devil as their sex educator, and because of this, they have mistaken ideas about sex. They think sin will make their sexual relationship better, but it does nothing of the kind. Instead, sin causes a marriage relationship to become unhealthy—and eventually to die.

Sin kills everything it touches. It never makes anything better. It always brings destruction, because "the wages of sin is death" (Rom. 6:23). The devil's purpose in tempting people to sin is simple. He wants "to steal, and to kill, and to destroy" them (John 10:10). Sin only devastates—it never helps anything.

The serpent says that pornography, and magazines such as *Playboy* and *Penthouse*, is just a harmless way to make your sex life better. In reality, he knows viewing pornography will destroy the intimacy and security that is essential to good sex by bringing another person into the relationship, even if that person only exists on the pages of a magazine. That *other* person has been invited into the thoughts of the husband or the wife, and when the thoughts of either partner are on anyone else, intimacy is lost.

By its very definition, intimacy is something special, something private. Sex should be the most intimate relationship on Earth, shared only between a husband and wife. Bringing someone else into that relationship, whether the person is real or imaginary, is a violation of that unique bond. In destroying the intimacy of sex, pornography destroys something very precious—and essential to—the sexual relationship.

Sexual sin also fatally wounds the marital relationship by causing feelings of rejection where there ought to be feelings of acceptance and affirmation. When a man insists pornography or some other form of sin will make sex more exciting, he is really telling his wife, *You are not good enough for me. You are not enough to turn me on. I need stimulation from looking at another woman in a magazine or movie before I can be in the mood for sex with you.* Rejection will not spice up anyone's sex life. It will create a huge wound in the heart of the woman, making her feel inferior and insecure. Those are not feelings that are conducive to good sex and true intimacy.

Men need to realize that pornography is unfair and unrealistic. It only portrays young, perfectly proportioned women who have been airbrushed to perfection—they appear to have no flaws. But such perfection does not exist—such beauty is fabricated. True beauty is found in the woman who has pledged herself—body and soul—to her husband.

Karen and I have been married over 30 years, and she is more beautiful to me now than she has ever been. I would never compare my wife's body to the body of any woman who has not sacrificed herself to bear and raise my children.

But beyond the damage that pornography does to a marriage and the pain it inflicts on a wife, it will eventually bring dissatisfaction to the husband. Why? The intensity of sexual sin must constantly be increased in order to achieve gratification. It's called the law of diminishing returns—and when it comes to pornography, the law dictates that the end result will be utter desolation. A wife may say, "I thought if he just looked at *Playboy* magazine then that would be enough for him. But after a while, he wanted to look at R-rated movies, and then he started to bring home X-rated movies. Now, the movies are not enough and he says we need to act out those things!"

Believing the serpent's lie that sin will help your sex life is the beginning of the end of your marriage.

Experimentation is the first step. If a man looks at something sexually shocking, he may justify it by saying, "Well, there is nothing wrong with that. It's exciting, so why not look again?" Then he looks again, but that excitement does not last for long. After a while, the things that had been so arousing are no longer arousing. What had been so shocking is no longer shocking at all. That *experimentation* has lead to *desensitization* and normal sexual feelings have died. More and more sin is then required to arouse any sexual response. This leads to the third step in the cycle, which is *escalation*. At this point, the devil convinces a person to begin *doing* those things he's been *seeing* in pornography. This is the *acting out* stage in the cycle.

This last stage brings tremendous destruction to a person's marriage and life. It is dangerous to even experiment with sexual sin because of where that sin will lead—death. If a man is thinking that a few racy movies will spice up his sex life, he should think again. Experimentation with pornography may seem harmless in the beginning, but it leads to total destruction in the end.

Bringing sin into any marriage will take a heavy toll. One man who had once been addicted to pornography shared how he had been delivered from that sin. He was then asked the question, "What has pornography cost you?" He answered, "Two marriages, and $70,000 in credit card bills." Sin did nothing to spice up this man's life. It cost him his marriage, not once but twice. It cost him dearly in the area of his finances. It cost him something that is very precious in the eyes of God. It cost him the opportunity to enjoy the gift of sex as God created it. And it cost him the wonderful experience of being fulfilled in that area of his life.

The best sex is pure sex. The best sex is sex within the marriage covenant, just as God designed. Those who turn their backs on sin and yield their sexuality to God's plan for their lives will experience the best sex. They will experience true fulfillment and discover the unending delights that only God can supply.

Lie #12: Sexual Sin Isn't Really Wrong if It Doesn't Hurt Anybody

This line is one of the most common lies in our society today and is used to justify all kinds of sin. "If I am not hurting anybody, then there is nothing wrong with what I am doing." Yet this argument has no basis in truth.

The truth is this: *Sin always hurts someone.* Let me say that another way: There is simply no such thing as a "victimless" sin. Sin will always hurt and bring death.

What's more, sin, in this case sexual sin, has infected even the Church. Doubtful? Consider this: There is a wonderful men's ministry called Promise Keepers that is dedicated to motivating men to become godly influences. The organization conducts rallies all across America and in other parts of the world. Tens of thousands of men have attended these rallies, and many of these men are Christians. One year, Promise Keepers conducted a survey during their events and asked: "When was the last time that you looked at pornography?" It was discovered that 50 percent of the men surveyed had viewed pornography within the very week that Promise Keepers' event was held.

I am not trying to single out men or overemphasize the prevalence of pornography—I am simply pointing out the unpleasant truth that pornography is a very serious problem in America today. It has become an epidemic and is affecting many families, including Christian families. In spite of all the devastation it is causing, the serpent continues to sell the idea that pornography doesn't hurt anyone, because it is a "private" sin. "I am not hurting anyone," a man may say. "This is not affecting anyone else, so what is so wrong with it?"

Many things are wrong with it. Let me repeat the well-known fact that pornography hurts women—both the woman who is objectified and the wife who is rejected. When the wife suffers, the marriage suffers. Then the family unit begins to suffer. Then the children feel the pain of their father's sin. And sooner or later, as the husband gets deeper and deeper into the porno pit, he will begin to feel the pain of having lost himself to a vice that has swallowed him whole. Clearly, "private" sin is a myth.

Another aspect of sin that makes it very harmful is this: *Sin separates us from God.* The Bible says:

> The Lord's hand is not shortened, that it cannot save; nor His ear heavy, that it cannot hear. But your iniquities have separated you from your God; and your sins have hidden His face from you, so that He will not hear (Isa. 59:1-2).

We know nothing can separate us from the *love* of God. But there is something that can separate us from *fellowship* with Him. There is something that can cause God to hide His face from us and not hear our prayers, and that "something" is sin.

When we sin, we can always go to Jesus and receive forgiveness—His blood is more than enough to cleanse us of any sin we commit. But when we willfully sin and hide it from God, when we choose not to bring it to Him for help and deliverance, that sin will separate us from God's presence and hinder us from hearing His voice. When we are out of fellowship with God, we are walking in darkness. Darkness will only lead to further sin, which will prevent us from walking in the power of His Spirit. The fruit of the Spirit will no longer characterize our lives (see Gal. 5:22-23). Instead of communicating love, peace and joy, we will communicate selfishness and fear. The darkness and damage of sin will cast a shadow on all our relationships.

Again—and I don't think I can emphasize this enough—there is no such thing as a "private" sin. Even if no one knows about it but God, the effects of sin will carry over into every area of our lives, and end up hurting those around us.

For the sake of illustration, imagine, if you will, two different scenarios. In one scenario, a man goes into a room in his home, closes the door and spends one hour in prayer and in God's Word. In the other scenario, a man goes into that room alone, closes the door and spends one hour viewing pornography. Now imagine that those two men step out of those rooms. What kind of a person will each one be? What kind of spiritual leader will each one be?

When a man has spent one hour looking at pornography, I guarantee you it will have an effect on him—on the way he treats the people in his life. He will have only one thing on his mind—and it will not be how he can bless his wife or his children. He will not be thinking about what he can give to his children or how he can serve his wife. He will be thinking only about himself and what he can get. He will want something from his wife that is wrong and unreasonable, and she will not be able to satisfy that lust. In the process, she will feel violated and used, because he will be treating her like an object, rather than like a human being who is created in the image of God.

I heard a minister make the observation that when a man has sex with his wife under the influence of pornography, he is really just having vaginal masturbation. That man is not loving or serving his wife. He's not sharing something intimate and precious with her; rather, he's using his wife to have an orgasm after he has been excited by looking at another woman. That is just plain selfish, and it is very harmful to the relationship.

Now what would the man do who had spent one hour alone with God, praying and studying God's Word. What kind of a person, husband and father will that man be?

After spending time with God, God's love, wisdom and power will be present in that man's life. He will leave that room with something to give, not with a mind to get something. He will be thinking about the people he loves and how he can bless them.

This will make him a husband who is completely different from the one who has been looking at pornography. It will also make him a very different role model for his children.

When a father has an attachment to a particular sin, especially if it's sexual in nature, he will set an incredibly negative example for his children, one that will pull them in the wrong direction. Children are far more influenced by the example that is lived out before them than by anything that is "said." Whether sin is spoken or unspoken, hidden or in plain view, children will be dramatically affected by that sin. If a man lives his life justifying sin and making excuses for iniquity, he should not be surprised if his children do the same. And not only that, sin also leaves a door open for demonic oppression to come into a home.

Every man must realize he is the priest and the doorkeeper of the home. If he is living a life of secret sin, he is inviting demonic oppression into his home, and his family will come under attack. Keep in mind that demons do not fight fairly. They go straight for the most vulnerable members: the children.

Bottom line: You cannot let sin in and keep the devil out.

Why? Because sin is Satan's rightful domain. When a man is looking at pornography or watching something on television that is inappropriate, he is allowing the devil an entrance into his home. He may think no one knows what he is doing. But while he is looking at pornography late at night, his children are likely to be harassed by demons as they try to sleep.

Scary stuff. And it all begins with "just one little peek."

So how do we protect ourselves from the schemes of the deceiver? We listen to the Holy Spirit. His voice is very gentle and sweet, yet it is unmistakable. It isn't difficult to sense when the Holy Spirit is grieved about something we are doing. And, when He begins to object to our actions and attitudes, we must listen to His voice and obey His promptings. We know when the Holy Spirit is prompting us to change the channel on the television or to look away from something that is inappropriate. God is not the least bit interested in looking at pornography. He is letting us know that He will not hang around if we choose to participate in sinful things.

If we choose to do something that grieves His Holy Spirit, it will cause His Spirit to stand at a distance from us. Definitely, we do not want that. We want His Spirit with us in everything we do. We need His guidance and His power to make it through this life.

So our course is clear: We must steer clear of sin. We must not allow sinful things in our lives—things like pornography that can cause a rift in our relationship with the Lord.

For myself, I have made the decision that when I am watching television, or whatever I do, I always ask this question: "Would I do this in the presence of God?" Would I watch golf on television in the presence of God? Absolutely. He is right there, watching it with me (He likes golf too, in case you didn't know!).

Would I have sex with my wife in the presence of God? Of course I would! God is not in the least offended by that because sex within the covenant of marriage is something wonderful He designed.

Would I look at pornography in the presence of God? Of course not. Sin always causes separation from God, and I do not want to do anything to drive His Holy Spirit from my life. I need Him in every area of my life. I need Him so that I can be the man He wants me to be—and the husband He created me to be. I need Him so that I can be the father He desires for me to be. I need Him in order to have the strength and power to walk out His purposes for my life.

And so do you.

Remember, sin will stop you from being the person God wants you to be. Sin will stop you from being the husband and father God wants you to be. Sin will rob you of the freedom you need to walk out God's purposes for your life.

Any voice that says otherwise is the voice of the serpent. So don't fall for the lie. Listen instead to the voice of the Spirit—and live in the truth.

PART III

the
conspiracy
unfolds

the conspiracy code

During the second World War, the Allied forces had a serious problem. The Nazis were using a secret code that even the most accomplished Allied cryptologists could not break. As a result, the enemy had a great advantage over us. Allied forces were unable to foresee enemy attacks, much less prepare for them, and the situation became more and more critical.

Thankfully, through a series of fortuitous events, the code finally was deciphered. That was the turning point in the conflict. Armed with knowledge of the enemy's tactics, Allied forces were able to prepare in advance for attacks and gain the advantage. Their knowledge of the enemy's code gave them the crucial information they needed to be victorious.

Much like those armies, we also are in a war. Our enemy, the devil, is trying to destroy us and thwart God's plans for our lives. His strategy hasn't changed in thousands of years—he consistently employs the same methods he has always used. And he uses those methods to attack us in every area of our lives, especially in the area of our sexuality.

The bad news is that the devil's method for drawing people into sin and darkness is an effective one.

But there is good news too.

The good news is that the enemy's "code" has been broken. This very effective and systematic strategy to attack and deceive people is what I call the devil's Conspiracy Code. We, like the Allied forces during World War II, can know the code, understand our enemy's tactics, be prepared and overcome his attacks every time.

We must acknowledge, first of all, that the devil is *always* working hard to lure us into sin. If we do not understand his strategy, he can keep us in a constant cycle of frustration, defeat and regret. If we fail to know *how* he works, we may gain the victory over sin for a while, only to fall back into defeat again and again.

However, when we understand the devil's strategy, we can overcome his attacks and live a life of constant victory.

Here's more good news: it is not difficult to understand this "Conspiracy Code." God's Word reveals quite clearly that there are six approaches the devil uses to deceive people and draw them into shame. We can stop an attack at any point along the way simply by recognizing the signposts on the road that leads from temptation to defeat.

Not surprisingly, the devil used these six steps when he duped Adam and Eve. By taking a closer look at what happened in the Garden of Eden, we can learn how to avoid falling into the same trap:

> Now the serpent was more cunning than any beast of the field which the Lord God had made. And he said to the woman, "Has God indeed said, 'You shall not eat of every tree of the garden'?" And the woman said to the serpent, "We may eat the fruit of the trees of the garden; but of the fruit of the tree which is in the midst of the garden, God has said, 'You shall not eat it, nor shall you touch it, lest you die.'" And the serpent said to the woman, "You will not surely die. For God knows that in the day you eat of it your eyes will be opened, and you will be like God, knowing good and evil."
>
> So when the woman saw that the tree was good for food, that it was pleasant to the eyes, and a tree desirable to make one wise, she took of its fruit and ate. She also gave to her husband with her, and he ate. Then the eyes of both of them were opened, and they knew that they were naked; and they sewed fig leaves

together and made themselves coverings. And they heard the sound of the Lord God walking in the garden in the cool of the day, and Adam and his wife hid themselves from the presence of the Lord God among the trees of the garden.

Then the Lord God called to Adam and said to him, "Where are you?" So he said, "I heard Your voice in the garden, and I was afraid because I was naked, and I hid myself." And He said, "Who told you that you were naked? Have you eaten from the tree of which I commanded you that you should not eat?" (Gen. 3:1–11).

This brief passage of Scripture reveals all six phases of the unfolding conspiracy. What can we learn from these verses?

Just how are we to thwart the plan of the enemy?

Read on and find out!

conspiracy step #1:
disguising his true identity

The devil did not appear to Eve as a big scary beast, with horns on his head and a pitchfork in his hand.

No.

The devil crept into the Garden disguised as a serpent. Why did he choose to appear in this form rather than that of a giraffe or a crocodile or a lion?

This passage tells us why.

It says that the serpent was "more cunning than any beast of the field." The word "cunning" means "stealthy" or "sly." The serpent, unlike other beings, had the ability to slide up next to its prey without begin noticed. The devil is sly like a serpent. He can sneak into our lives and be present without our realizing it.

A few years ago I had the opportunity to learn firsthand about how "cunning" serpents can be. While playing golf in Albuquerque, I happened to hit a ball into the rough. As I went to retrieve my ball, I noticed a sign warning of rattlesnakes in the area. I didn't see any snakes, so I took another step. A rattling sound came from the bushes. I hesitated; then, all went silent. So, I just took one more step. This time I heard multiple rattles. The choice ahead of me seemed clear at that point: *Die, or forget about getting my golf ball!* I'm sure you can guess what I did—I quickly and quietly walked away. Though I never saw a rattlesnake that day, the truth is, those snakes were there.

Serpents can silently creep up without making their presence known—and that is exactly how the devil operates. When he comes into our lives to tempt us, he does not draw attention to himself or reveal his true identity. He wants to keep us focused on the deception and temptation. Remember how he kept Eve focused on the forbidden fruit and his lies? She had no idea she was being enticed by the devil.

That's because he is the master of disguise. The devil knows that if he showed up in a shocking red suit, sporting horns on his head and dragging a pointy tail, we would never allow him entrance into our lives. Just imagine him knocking on your door. "Hello, I'm Satan. Please allow me to come inside," he asks politely. "I have all kinds of tricks up my sleeve that will bring destruction into your life. If you will spend some time with me, I promise you will never be the same."

How long would it take for you to slam the door in his face and lock it?

He knows that. So, our enemy masquerades as something harmless. He tries to lure us away from God by disguising himself as someone innocuous. He even will pretend to be someone who is there to help us, perhaps even as someone who has been "sent by God." In fact, the Bible tells us Satan can transform himself into an *angel of light:*

> Such are false apostles, deceitful workers, transforming themselves into apostles of Christ, and no wonder! For Satan himself transforms himself into an angel of light. Therefore it is no great thing if his ministers also transform themselves into ministers of righteousness, whose end will be according to their works (2 Cor. 11:13-15).

The devil realizes we will not *knowingly* follow an evil person—and he also knows we will be inclined to follow a person who appears to be a "minister of righteousness" who is there to *help us with our problems.*

When Satan came to Eve in the Garden of Eden, he did not introduce himself by saying, "Hey, Eve, I'm Lucifer, the fallen angel who was kicked out of heaven." No. He presented himself as a harmless, helpful being. It seemed as if he just *happened* to be at the right place at the right time when Eve was studying that tree. Though he was there for all the wrong reasons, he was friendly and chatty. And he was ready and willing to assist Eve with her dilemma.

He masterfully kept Eve's attention focused on his temptation—and off his character and motives. He kept her thinking about the lies he was spinning rather than the truth of what God had said.

The devil didn't care about gaining her *affection* as much as he cared about gaining her *defection*. In other words, it was not important to the devil that she follow *him*, as long as he could prevent her from following *God*. His intention is no different in our lives.

Satan's Favorite Disguise

It's true that Satan likes to present himself as an angel of light, but he has another disguise that he uses far more often.

Us!

That's right. If we are not mindful to listen to the voice of the Holy Spirit at all times, he can use you and me to be his mouthpiece. The devil often persuades trusted believers to advise others to do things that are contrary to God's will. Perhaps you have had a family member or close friend encourage you to do something that was not in keeping with the direction God had given you. Perhaps unknowingly you have been the one to give bad advice to a close friend. The bottom line here is that if we are ignorant of the devil's devices, we can be susceptible to his strategy.

The apostle Peter fell into this very trap.

The enemy influenced his thoughts, then tried to use him to influence Jesus to walk away from God's will. What's more, Peter fell prey to this strategy of the enemy only moments after speaking words of revelation that came directly from God the Father!

He asked His disciples, saying, "Who do men say that I, the Son of Man, am?" So they said, "Some say John the Baptist, some Elijah, and others Jeremiah or one of the prophets." He said to them, "But who do you say that I am?" And Simon Peter answered and said, "You are the Christ, the Son of the living God." Jesus answered and said to him, "Blessed are you, Simon Bar-Jonah, for flesh and blood has not revealed this to you, but My Father who is in heaven" (Matt. 16:13–17).

The Father in heaven had revealed Jesus' true identity to Peter. In this instance, God used Peter as His mouthpiece in the earth to proclaim Jesus as "the Christ, the Son of the living God."

And, immediately after proclaiming this truth, Peter spoke words that were straight from the devil!

When Jesus began to prepare His disciples for the fact that as the Christ He would have to suffer a horrible death on the cross, Peter did not listen to what the Holy Spirit had to say about it. He did not even listen to what Jesus had to say. Instead, Peter listened to the enemy. He took Jesus aside and said, "Far be it from You, Lord; this shall not happen to You!"

But was this thought to resist the plan of God really Peter's idea?

No. Peter had been influenced by the devil. We know that because Jesus "turned and said to Peter, 'Get behind Me, Satan! You are an offense to Me, for you are not mindful of the things of God, but the things of men'" (Matt. 16:23).

Now, when Jesus said this to Peter, did He actually mean that Peter was "Satan"? Of course not. Jesus recognized that the devil had slithered up and whispered those words into Peter's mind. So, Jesus addressed Satan directly.

Now I want you to understand, the devil could not control or even know what Peter was thinking. However, he could, and did, whisper thoughts to him. I'm sure Peter didn't realize he was listening to the enemy. He merely had an idea about the way things should be, and he voiced that idea.

In the same way, the devil can introduce thoughts into *our* minds. If we are not careful, we will think that those ideas are coming from our own minds, or even from God Himself, and we will not recognize the true source.

Essentially there are only three ways thoughts originate. They come from God, our own minds or the devil.

If a thought is coming from the devil, we have to resist that thought. If he whispers an idea into our minds and convinces us it is from God or part of our own thinking, he has succeeded in the first step of his conspiracy code. We must learn to distinguish the source of our thoughts.

Apparently Peter couldn't tell the difference.

In the account we just read, the Holy Spirit spoke to Peter and Peter listened. But when Satan suddenly spoke to Peter, Peter listened to him as well. How could that happen? How could Peter go so quickly from listening to the voice of God to listening to the voice of the devil?

Jesus gives us the answer in the very next verse when He said to Peter, "You are an offense to Me, for you are not mindful of the things of God, but the things of men." Here, Jesus points out that Peter's self-interest opened him up to hearing the voice of the devil. The bottom line is, Peter was thinking more about what Peter wanted than about what God wanted. He was more interested in an outcome that seemed right to him than in the outcome God had declared. Peter's reaction was *selfish*.

Selfishness is the way Satan gains an entrance into our thinking as well. Through selfishness, self-interest and self-promotion, the devil is able to get our minds off God's priorities and on to our own desires. Then he has an open door to come in and contaminate our thinking with his lies. He convinces us that those lies are coming from our own minds, or even from God.

So, how do we tell the difference?

Well, thoughts from God are easy to discern. They are always full of love, full of peace and full of truth. And His thoughts are always consistent with His Word. We can easily recognize the voice of God because His voice is loving and kind, and His voice always is in agreement with His Word.

On the other hand, when the devil brings an idea to our minds it will be contrary to God's Word. The devil tries to introduce ideas that contradict what God has said. He did that to Peter. God had said through the Old Testament prophets that the Christ would have to suffer and die—it was written in Scripture. But the devil whispered something contrary to Peter. Peter ignorantly agreed with the idea introduced by the devil rather than evaluating it in light of God's Word.

The devil contradicts God's Word, and tempts us away from God's ways and purposes. He plants seeds of doubt in our minds and causes us to question what God has said. He whispers rebellious thoughts in our minds, while trying to make us believer such thoughts are our own.

But how do we sense his influence? Remember, we are at war with an enemy who disguises himself. He presents himself as an angel of light, a minister of righteousness, a dear friend. He disguises his thoughts as our own so that we will embrace his ideas and act on them.

The Bible tells us how to recognize his strategy and discern his tactics as we seek to overcome him.

> For the weapons of our warfare are not carnal but mighty in God for pulling down strongholds, casting down arguments and every high thing that exalts itself against the knowledge of God, bringing every thought into captivity to the obedience of Christ (2 Cor. 10:4-5).

This battle is a spiritual battle that can be won only with spiritual weapons. This verse tells us we must treat "enemy" thoughts like enemy warriors—we must take them captive. We are to seize any thoughts that are not from God and bring them to Jesus. Every thought is to be measured against the Word. It's up to us to make our thinking "obey" and come into line with what God has said.

If we fail to take captive the thoughts the devil introduces into our minds, those thoughts will eventually take *us* captive.

There may not be a demon behind every bush, but the devil is very real, and he does seek to destroy us and our families. He wants to steal, kill and destroy what God has planned for our lives. If we choose to ignore that fact, we will be helpless against his attacks. God tells us in the Bible that we should not be ignorant of the devil's devices, "lest Satan should take advantage of us" (2 Cor. 2:11). God intends for us to know how the devil operates so that we can overcome his schemes and walk in victory.

Yet as believers in Jesus Christ, however, we are to be more aware of God and His presence in our lives than of what the devil is doing. God's redeeming power and His love should be more real to us than any attack of the devil. In order for that to be the case, we must spend time with God and His Word so that we can know Him intimately. God loves us and desires to be near to us. As we focus on Him and what He is doing rather than on what the devil is doing, we find a place of balance between the two extremes of ignoring the devil entirely or making everything about him.

That is the place God wants us to walk.

When we know God and have a relationship with Him, we can learn to recognize His voice. Jesus said that His sheep "follow him, for they know his voice." His sheep "will by no means follow a stranger, but will flee from him, for they do not know the voice of strangers" (John 10:4-5).

When we belong to Jesus, we can distinguish the difference between His voice and the voice of the enemy. The Bible tells us God has given us a spiritual gift to help us know which spirit is speaking to us. This gift is called "discerning of spirits" (1 Cor. 12:10). Discerning of spirits is the supernatural ability to discern the nature of the spiritual entities around us. When this gift is in operation, we can discern, or *just know* inside our hearts, when something is not of God. This *knowing* enables us to resist that "thing" and refuse to allow it to gain a foothold in our thinking.

Countering Conspiracy Step #1

As we discussed, part of the devil's conspiracy plan is to disguise himself and often pass off his lies as our own thoughts. So what's our best defense against this kind of attack? It's to stay alert, know God's Word and learn to recognize the voice of the Holy Spirit so that we are able to discern when the lies of the enemy are trying to creep in.

God's Word is the standard by which we need to measure every thought. As we spend time with Him in prayer and in His Word, we will come to know Him, and we will also learn to readily recognize thoughts that do not line up with His Word and His will. We can immediately take thoughts captive and stop the cunning attacks of the enemy against us.

His conspiracy to deceive us will fail.

conspiracy step #2:
isolating and attacking

When the enemy first slithered into the Garden, Adam and Eve had a right relationship with God. They walked and talked daily with the God who had given them a perfect paradise in which to live. They were also in right relationship with one another and free from fear or shame.

How could the devil possibly draw them away from the loving God who had blessed them in so many ways? By *isolating* Eve.

In Genesis 3:1, we notice that the serpent did not approach the man and woman together. Here's why: He knew Eve would not be as vulnerable if Adam were with her. He knew he had to catch her when she was alone.

Eve's first mistake was allowing the devil to single her out and talk to her in that way. She did not have to be alone at that moment. Her husband was nearby and she could have included him in the conversation. We know this because she turned to Adam immediately after eating of the forbidden fruit and offered it to him. She could have turned to Adam *before* eating of the fruit. She could have talked to him and given him the opportunity to speak into that situation. But the serpent got to Eve while she was alone—and by the time Adam became involved, Eve had already sinned.

Adam and Eve also could have included God in their conversation in this situation since they were accustomed to talking to Him at that time of day. We know this is true because immediately after Adam and Eve had eaten the forbidden fruit, God approached them. The Bible says, "they heard the sound of the Lord God walking in the garden in the cool of the day" (Gen. 3:8).

Before they sinned, Adam and Eve had a close relationship with God—they spent time with Him on a regular basis. Had they talked to God about the life-altering decision they were considering, He would have reminded them of the truth. He would have exposed Satan's lies for what they were. But because Adam and Eve allowed themselves to be isolated from God and from one another, they were more vulnerable to temptation.

That is one key element in the devil's strategy to deceive people—to isolate them before attacking. We are far more susceptible to temptation when we are by ourselves.

The Danger of Isolation

The devil's goal is to lure us away from the truth. Having godly people around us is a built-in deterrent to his plan to draw us into sin. It's next to impossible for him to get to us when we are in right relationship with God and when we are surrounded by other believers.

So before launching an attack against us, the devil works hard to isolate us. We must be aware of this and guard against it. The fact is that the world in which we live makes it easy for the devil to isolate people and draw them into sin. In our culture, people are always on the go away from home and have easy access to the Internet, movies and television. Remember, Satan works in the darkness. When a person is in a chat room, surfing sites on the Internet or viewing television alone, the devil is in a position to tempt that person and pull him or her into sin.

All the men I have known who have struggled with addiction to pornography became addicted in an environment of isolation. Though it may be difficult to believe, it has been discovered that 70 percent of the pornography viewed in this country is viewed at work between the hours of 9:00 and 5:00. Men are often isolated in their offices—whether home offices or workplace offices—with their computer (complete with Internet access and DVD player). In such environments, there is rarely any accountability.

A woman can become just as isolated and subject to temptation while watching soap operas or reading racy novels. The devil can pull her into a fantasy world when there is no one present to pull her back into reality.

Children also can become isolated and fall into temptation. Parents must be diligent and not allow their children to isolate themselves in a room alone with a television or computer.

The devil knows that if he can isolate a man, woman or child, then that man, woman or child can become vulnerable to temptation.

Recently, I heard a very sad story that illustrates how devastating it can be when a young person becomes isolated.

A 15-year-old girl got involved in an online relationship with a young man she met through a chat room. Their online relationship became more and more involved until the young girl decided she was "in love" and she wanted to meet this person. Though it is hard to imagine, *somehow* this girl convinced her mother to drive her to a neighboring state to see this 15-year-old boy.

When they arrived, this young girl and her mother were in for the shock of their lives! They discovered this person was not a young man at all. "He" was in fact an older *lesbian woman.*

Isolated in a chat room, this vulnerable 15-year-old girl had been deceived and had "fallen in love with" a lesbian, 10 years her senior. If only the story ended there, that would be bad enough—but it doesn't!

At first, this young girl was upset. Next, she was confused. But, then she thought, *Wait a minute. I fell in love with this person. This person is a woman. Therefore, I am in love with a woman. Therefore, I must be a lesbian.*

And, as appalling as it is, that 15-year-old girl ended up running away with that lesbian woman, who could only be described as a pedophile!

This heartbreaking story exemplifies the damage that can occur when a child is allowed to surf the Web without parental supervision.

Parents must insist that the computer and the television be in an open area of the house where everyone can see what is being viewed. Children may ask, "Don't you trust me?" Parents should confidently reply, "No, I do not because I do not trust myself."

The truth of the matter is, none of us is immune to temptation.

I will never be so foolish as to tell myself that I cannot fall into sin simply because I am a minister, or because I have known the Lord for a number of years. Not one of us is spiritually strong enough to face the devil alone for an extended period of time. So if we allow ourselves to be isolated, we are setting ourselves up for a fall.

Two or More Bring Power

Jesus understood how isolation weakens our resistance to sin. When He sent His disciples out to minister, Jesus did not send them out one by one, but "two by two" (Luke 10:1).

I believe He did this because He understood that isolation invites temptation. These disciples were men—and a man who is alone is an easy target for the devil. I believe Jesus knew that having two men take a journey together would greatly reduce the chances of any one of His disciples falling into sexual immorality.

We are much more likely to resist temptation when there is someone else present to hold us accountable.

God does not want us to be alone. He knows there is safety in numbers, and He also knows there is potential power when two or more are together. When Jesus was teaching His disciples about prayer, He said to them:

Again I say to you that if two of you agree on earth concerning anything that they ask, it will be done for them by My Father in heaven. For where two or three are gathered together in My name, I am there in the midst of them (Matt. 18:19-20).

We are more powerful together than alone. Jesus made it clear that power is available to us when we pray in agreement with others.

When God created Adam, He said, "It is not good that man should be alone" (Gen. 2:18). God knows when we become isolated we become easy prey for the enemy.

The world in which we live, however, makes it easier and easier for people to become isolated from each other. Through all kinds of media, the devil is pushing more and more people into darkness and isolation. He is hammering men, women and children with sexual temptation—and when they fall into sin, it is nearly always in an environment of isolation. We absolutely must make up our minds that we will not allow ourselves to become easy prey for the devil.

It is also important to recognize that being isolated can be more than just the physical condition of being alone. Isolation can be an *attitude* of refusing to be accountable. An attitude of isolation says, "No one needs to know or has a right to know what I am doing. I do not need to be accountable to anyone else—it is nobody's business but my own."

This attitude will help the devil achieve success every time. It becomes easy for him to get to people who are sporting this attitude. Alone in the darkness, they become subject to his control.

Let's make up our minds that we will not live in isolation—that we won't give control of our lives over to the devil.

Men, support, pray with and help each other! When you are accountable to other men, you can go to someone and confess if you are having sexual struggles. A godly person can listen and pray for you to be healed and forgiven. You can be strengthened and helped by the presence of faith.

In the same way, women, seek out other women to help you deal with the issues you face. You as women often are better able to help each other than men are able to help other men. It's easier for you to be compassionate and pray with and support one another.

There is tremendous power available in this type of agreement.

Regardless of our gender, God wants us to work together in this life. He wants us to be in fellowship with one another, because such togetherness brings safety, encouragement and strength. It enables us to work together to win the battle!

Countering Conspiracy Step #2

The enemy conspires to get us off by ourselves, where he can pick us off one by one. We can thwart this attack simply by refusing to allow ourselves to be isolated. That means:

- Communicating honestly with our spouse
- Staying in fellowship with and being accountable to other believers
- Sharing one another's burdens in prayer
- Living openly and honestly before God and each other

By doing these things, we protect our lives and inoculate ourselves from the devil's conspiracy to destroy us.

conspiracy step #3:
disarming and then attacking his prey

God has given us powerful weapons with which to combat the devil. We must recognize what these weapons of warfare are and utilize their power in order to overcome the devices of the enemy.

Doing this is much like harnessing nuclear power. Within the tiny nucleus of an atom there is an amazing amount of power just waiting to be released. Once that power is released, it can destroy everything in sight. The power within that atom is so great that most of our puny minds would have a hard time comprehending it. But if we knew how to tap into that power, even though we didn't fully understand how or why it worked, we could use it.

Well, the Word of God is very much like nuclear power. And most of us really cannot fathom how the power that is within God's Word works. Nonetheless, if we learn how to use it, we can do tremendous damage to the kingdom of darkness.

The devil understands this fact. He knows that he cannot stand up against the Word of God. It is just too powerful for him. So what does he do?

He tries to disarm us by getting us to lay aside the Word. In fact, the very first words the devil spoke to Eve challenged the words of God. He came to Eve and asked her, "Has God indeed said?" (Gen. 3:1). If we were to paraphrase this, it might sound something like this: "Hmm . . . You don't say? Well, are you sure God really said that? Maybe you misunderstood. I think there's been some mistake here. God really couldn't have said that, could He?"

The devil challenged the word of God because he knew the word had the power to defeat him—and he is still using that same tactic today for the same reason. He knows he has no chance to defeat us if we are armed with the Word of God. So he challenges it, contradicts it and tries to convince us to put it down.

The Power of the Word

Many Christians do not fully realize the power that is available to them in God's Word. His Word is so much more than writing on a page—it is alive and full of supernatural power. This is how the letter to the Hebrews describes it:

> For the word of God is living and powerful, and sharper than any two-edged sword, piercing even to the division of soul and spirit, and of joints and marrow, and is a discerner of the thoughts and intents of the heart. And there is no creature hidden from His sight, but all things are naked and open to the eyes of Him to whom we must give account (Heb. 4:12–13).

The Word of God is sharper than *any* two-edged sword. It can cut through all of the devil's lies and deception. So it's little wonder Satan works so hard to get us to lay down God's Word. It is a powerful, powerful weapon against him.

"The sword of the Spirit" is the weapon Jesus Himself used in His confrontation with the devil. In Matthew 4, we read about how the devil wanted to stop Jesus from fulfilling the plans of God for His life on this earth. So he attacked Jesus.

What did Jesus do? He used God's Word to stop the devil in his tracks.

He didn't call in a legion of angels—though He could have.

He didn't perform a miracle to scare the devil away—though He was perfectly capable of doing so.

No, Jesus simply *spoke the Word of God*, and the devil simply had to leave.

The devil was using half-truths and manipulation to try to tempt Jesus to sin. He even quoted Scriptures in his efforts to trip up Jesus. But the devil was no match for Jesus. Every time the devil came up with a new temptation, Jesus just shot back with the Word: "It is written . . ." (Luke 4:4).

The Word was effective in defeating the lies and deception of the enemy, for the Bible tells us that the devil gave up—he left (see Luke 4:13).

When we speak the Word of God, the devil must leave us, too.

God's Word is just as powerful for us today as it was that day when Jesus defeated the devil with it. That is the reason the devil tries to take that "sword" away from us—or at least to make sure it has no real place in our lives. He knows that if we put down the Word, we become easy prey for his attacks. When we speak the Word, there is no way he can lead us into sin and defeat.

The Word of God is powerful enough to break *every* area of bondage. This means God's Word can even demolish addictions that have had a foothold in a person's life for years.

I discovered this myself.

Early exposure to sin and pornography had caused many problems and struggles in my life. After I married Karen, I was really trying to live for God, but I could not get the victory in the area of my thought life. I lived in a constant cycle of temptation, failure, regret and defeat. Although I knew I had been called into ministry, I wondered how God could ever use someone like me, who was trapped in such a cycle of failure.

One day, I picked up a little book about scriptural meditation, and what I read changed my life forever. That little book taught me about the power available to us when we meditate on God's Word. It was written by a man who had sold pornography as a child and struggled with that sin during his adult life. Even after knowing the Lord and serving as the president of a Bible college, he had not been able to break free from that sin until he learned the vital importance of biblical meditation.

I, too, quickly discovered that *meditation in God's Word is the only way to overcome sexual sin.*

Cold showers will not do it.

Crying and repenting for the millionth time will not do it.

It is a battle in the mind, not the hormones or the genitals. And the mind can be set free only by the power of God's Word.

Regardless of our addiction or sexual bondage, God's Word is able to free us. Though we may not fully understand how this power works, still we can unleash the power of God's Word and see the chains of sin fall away.

And I am not the only one to discover this power.

One of the most physically disciplined men I have ever met came to me for help at one time. He was a well-respected, high-ranking military man. This man seemed very "together" in every area of his life—certainly not the kind of person who would be controlled by anything. Yet he was addicted to pornography, and his addiction was about to cost him his marriage and his job.

"I am helpless," he confessed. "I look at pornography all the time. It is all I think about. It controls my sex life, and it is affecting my marriage in a very negative way. I am afraid that I will lose everything because of this sin, but I cannot stop. What am I to do?"

I talked to him about the power in God's Word and told him that he needed to meditate on the Scriptures. He agreed to do that and went home.

One week later he called me to say he had spent that week totally free from sexual addiction. He reported that *his freedom had come immediately when he began to meditate in the Word of God!*

We must understand that God's Word is much more than mere words in a book!

God's Word is living and powerful. It is sharper than any two-edged sword.

When we tap into the Word, we are tapping into something powerful enough to overcome the devil in *every* circumstance.

I want you to realize that the Word will set you free! It has the power to break strongholds in any area of your life, not only in the area of sexuality. Meditation on the Word of God infuses our spirits and minds with a supernatural life that breaks the power of sin.

And that is not the only thing God's Word will do. The first psalm talks about the many blessings that come from meditating on the Scriptures:

Blessed is the man who walks not in the counsel of the ungodly, nor stands in the path of sinners, nor sits in the seat of the scornful; but his delight is in the law of the Lord, and in His law he meditates day and night. He shall be like a tree planted by the rivers of water, that brings forth its fruit in its season, whose leaf also shall not wither; and whatever he does shall prosper (Ps. 1:1-3).

This passage of Scripture describes a man who meditates in the Word of God "day and night." In other words, when he wakes up in the morning, he feeds his spirit with God's truth and thinks about it all day.

The word "meditate" means to "ruminate"—or *to turn it over and over in the mind, and digest it.* When we do that, the Word goes down deep into our spirits and changes us on the inside. After meditating on God's Word, we are armed and ready to do battle when temptation strikes.

For example, you may be watching television when an image suddenly flashes across the screen and starts to pull you into lust or fantasy. At that moment, the devil is subtly trying to introduce sinful thoughts to your mind. If you try to resist him with your own thoughts, you will lose. Your thoughts simply are not powerful enough against the devil. He is better at this than you are. He will wear you out until you finally succumb to his temptation.

But God's Word is far more powerful than the devil's thoughts. When you have been meditating on God's Word, His truth will rise up inside you and put the thoughts of the enemy to flight.

God's Word *is* just like nuclear power!

I know this is true, because I have seen its power working in my own life. Until I learned to meditate on God's Word, I lived in constant sexual defeat and condemnation. But when I began to meditate on the Word of God and put His thoughts into my spirit, I was instantly set free.

Countering Conspiracy Step #3

The devil has always attacked God's Word as a part of his conspiracy to defeat us. The best way to counter that attack is to pull out the sword of God's Word daily. Do not allow yourself to be disarmed.

Put your faith in the Word of God, and refuse to let the devil cast doubt on it. Begin every day by putting God's Word into your thoughts, even if it is only one Scripture verse. Then meditate on that Word, and allow it to take root in your heart and mind. (More about this in chapter 22, where we'll take an in-depth look at biblical meditation.)

At the first sign of temptation, that Word inside you will rise up with supernatural power and overcome the thoughts of the devil. The Word is your weapon—the "nuclear" weapon that can destroy every lie of the devil's conspiracy.

conspiracy step #4:
focusing on the forbidden fruit and camouflaging the pain of sin

The devil likes to glamorize the forbidden fruit of sin. He wants to focus our attention on the "fun" we will have if we eat that fruit. At the same time, he conceals the actual aftermath of sin. He tries to convince us, just as he did Eve, that pain and death will not be the final outcome of sin.

The devil works hard to make sin look good.

Only after we take a bite of the forbidden fruit do we start to see the truth. By then, the devastation has already begun and the damage is done.

We must keep in mind at all times that the devil is a liar and the father of lies. Accuracy just is not his "gig." He will tell us anything we want to hear in order to draw us into his kingdom of darkness.

You've got to realize that the devil studies us carefully in order to pinpoint our weaknesses. He is able to create a tailor-made rationale in an effort to convince us there is nothing wrong with the sin we may be tempted to commit. If we want to believe adultery is acceptable, he will come up with a compelling way to justify it in our minds. He has mastered the art of "helping" us believe sin is really the best thing for our lives.

This is the next step in his conspiracy to lead us away from God and into disobedience.

The Illusion of Sin

This is exactly what the devil did to Eve. He focused her attention on the forbidden fruit, making it seem very attractive to her. He convinced Eve that sinning would be a good thing: "So when the woman saw that the tree was good for food, that it was pleasant to the eyes, and a tree desirable to make one wise, she took of its fruit and ate" (Gen. 3:6).

The devil made the fruit look very appealing to Eve—and it may well have been quite pleasant to look at. What we can learn from this is that on the surface, sin does not always appear ugly and destructive. The devil has a way of making sin look good. He likes to keep our attention focused on that illusion, and at the same time convince us that God has forbidden this sin because He is withholding something good from us.

Of course, the devil is a liar.

That fruit Eve ate was not good in any sense of the word. It was not good for food. It was deadly. It was poisonous. The very day Eve ate of that fruit, her physical body began to die. God had created her body to live forever, free of sickness or pain. The process of death, however, began the minute Eve ate of that fruit. Rather than making her wise, the forbidden fruit brought confusion into Eve's life. After she had eaten it, she became disoriented. Her mind was so darkened that she hid herself from God—the God she had talked to openly every day of her life, the God who had given her everything.

Was she thinking about all the wonderful ways God had blessed her life that day she ate of the fruit? It's doubtful.

The devil never draws attention to the goodness of God. Why? If we start to think about all the wonderful things God has done, that forbidden fruit of sin will no longer look so appealing. When we look around at the wonders of His creation, when we take a moment to thank Him for all His tremendous blessings in our lives and marvel at

His goodness, we soon forget about the forbidden fruit! When we start to worship and praise Him, sin loses its ability to ensnare us.

So what does the devil do?

He attempts to distract us from recognizing and remembering all God's blessings. He tries to focus our attention on things God has said we must stay away from. In order to make that fruit look more enticing, the devil will tell us any lie he thinks we'll buy.

The entertainment industry makes sin look inviting, pleasant and good. The most beautiful people in the world are seen on screen—doing anything they want without negative consequences. The message sent is "You can live your life without moral constraints, and benefit from it, rather than be destroyed by it." This has had devastating effects on our culture and society.

Now, I enjoy good entertainment as much as anyone, but the fact is, Hollywood seems to have perfected the art of portraying sin as glamorous. When people watch a sitcom on TV or go to a movie, they rarely see the pain and death that are the true results of sin.

Consider the popular movie *Titanic*. You may be familiar with the romantic story. A young man and woman meet on the ship. She poses nude for him as he draws her and then they have sex—all this after knowing each other for a few short hours. The guy dies when the ship sinks, and the girl goes on to marry another man. She spends the rest of her life living in a fantasy world, pining way for this man she had the brief affair with while on the Titanic. She never gives her heart fully to her husband, which means he spent his life married to a woman who did not really love him. Because of sin, she has been robbed of the blessings of married love, and her husband is missing out as well.

This enticing story, of course, was wrapped up with pretty ribbons so that it appeared glamorous, romantic and beautiful. Granted, the artistry and expertise that went into making that movie were top-notch.

Still, the message in the movie was very wrong: Illicit sex is wonderful and brings tremendous benefits.

The truth is, any girl who meets a stranger on a ship and has sex with him several hours later has a very good chance of becoming pregnant, and/or contracting a disease.

Still, in spite of what the entertainment industry shows us, the wages of sin is always death. Death comes in the form of sexually transmitted diseases, drug and alcohol addictions, pornography, violence and divorce. These evils are destroying millions of lives. But, does the media ever show that side of sin?

Do they write into the script a scenario of a beautiful woman who is not only sleeping around with multiple partners, but is also suffering from a sexually transmitted disease that is killing her as well as putting at risk the lives of her sexual partners?

Do they ever talk about a friend who had an abortion and explain that she has experienced mental and emotional problems as a result?

Do the comedy shows ever portray sexually active, promiscuous young girls contracting a disease that will destroy their chances of ever having children?

No. And it's not likely to happen any time soon because the devil doesn't want anyone talking about the true consequences of sin. He wants to camouflage the pain that sin brings and make it look "pleasant" to us. His advertising arm, the entertainment industry, has done amazing work for him. Now, to be fair, some of the folks in Hollywood may be unaware the devil has enlisted them in his conspiracy to make sin seem like harmless fun. If so, they need to wake up and realize that they have a huge influence in our nation. They have the ability to speak to an enormous audience. If we're part of that audience—and most of us are—we must be acutely aware of what images and messages we allow into our minds. Young people and adults alike need to ask themselves, "What is the message in the music I am listening to? What message is this show sending?" The things we allow into our minds have a powerful influence on our thinking. They will affect our attitudes and eventually our behavior as well.

Sexual sin always brings heartache, pain and devastation into the lives of those who eat that forbidden fruit. God has warned us about that in His Word. He has given us all the information we need to crack the devil's code of deception and counter his subterfuge.

Countering Conspiracy Step #4

When we know God and know His Word, we can avoid being ensnared in the devil's trap. We must do the following to counter his conspiracy:

• Remind ourselves that God's ways are the best ways
• Believe God's warnings about sin
• Refuse to listen to the deception that sin is fun and glamorous
• Understand that sin always will steal, kill and destroy us

With the light of Christ and His Word, we can see right through the devil's camouflage and refuse to take a bite from the forbidden fruit of sin.

conspiracy step #5:
brainwashing people and destroying god's purpose for their lives

---

Sin is very much like a Trojan horse. It may look fairly harmless at the outset, but it actually carries a lot of unexpected visitors!

Sin has a way of serving as an entry point for the devil. Once sin has been invited in, the gate of the mind is opened to all manner of deception and wrong thinking.

When the devil has isolated and disarmed us and then convinced us to sin, he has succeeded in sneaking his Trojan horse into our lives. This sets us up for the next step in his conspiracy—brainwashing us with falsehood and deception.

The devil will make short work of downloading lies into our mind until our way of thinking has changed. This is how he gains control in our life and stops God's plans for us from being fulfilled.

We see the evidence of this in the story of Adam and Eve. Before they sinned, Adam and Eve walked before God without fear or shame. In other words, their thinking was "right"— they were walking in truth. As soon as they ate that forbidden fruit, however, their thinking became confused and darkened. Suddenly, their thoughts were full of fear and shame. They believed their sexuality was shameful—and that they needed to hide themselves from God and one another. Yet Adam and Eve would not have been entertaining thoughts of fear or shame had they not eaten the forbidden fruit. Once they opened the door to sin, deception came in and the devil began his process of brainwashing.

You know the end of the story—they didn't live out their lives in the Garden of Eden or experience the complete blessing of God.

That is how the devil's conspiracy works. As soon as we grab the forbidden fruit of sin, he starts telling us things that will drive us further into darkness. He hopes to make us believe that there is something wrong with us, and that God could never love us because of the way we are or because of what we have done.

Perhaps you've heard some of his lies . . .

"God is the enemy," he whispers. "You'd better be afraid of Him. He no longer loves you. It is too late for God to ever work in your life again."

This could be labeled "Brainwashing 101."

If people continue to sin, they give the devil more opportunities to bring condemnation and to fill their mind with his lies. If people sin deliberately over a long period of time, they will eventually reach a point where their minds have been totally deceived. I call this "Advanced Brainwashing."

Satan's Advanced Brainwashing Course

When people reach this stage, they become convinced that they do not need God in their lives. They come to view God's laws as moral shackles that separate them from the source of their "happiness." Such people begin to believe that God, rather than sin, is the real problem.

Brainwashed people may decide there is no God, and therefore there are no rules. In their mind, sin then is just an inherent part of human nature, so they rationalize, "Why not just go ahead and do what comes *naturally?*"

While sin is part of fallen human nature—humanity without God— it is not to be part of *our* lives.

It's alarming to realize how many people in our culture have signed up for this advanced brainwashing course! Many people have become convinced that they do not need God, and they have given themselves over to sin. The results have been catastrophic.

As a pastor, I have witnessed many tragic instances of this pattern of destruction. Some of the most heartbreaking examples involve people who have yielded to sexual sin, which has resulted in advanced deception in their thinking. Consider two married people who commit adultery, claiming God told them it was His will for them to have this sinful relationship. You know they have been deceived. When they honestly believe God has revealed to them that He is going to kill both of their spouses so that they can marry each other without the scandal of divorce—you know the devil has moved in and set up housekeeping!

As hard as it may be to believe, this actually happened!

How could people be so deceived?

It's a *process* that begins when we sin—and thereby open the door to the devil. Once we have rejected the commandments of God and His Word, the devil has an open invitation to download his viruses into our minds. If we start to believe his lies, more wrong thinking and false beliefs are poured in our minds until advanced brainwashing has erased our knowledge of God.

This happened to a man who had been a dear friend of mine, and a brother in the Lord. Not only that, but he had been a leader in the church and at one time a very important spiritual influence in my life. I had attended Bible studies with this man. He had ministered to me, prayed with me and taught me the things of God.

But a day came when I received a phone call and he informed me he was leaving his wife and three young daughters. He had decided to follow a lifestyle of pornography and promiscuity.

My friend had been introduced to this kind of sin through his boss. He had gone to work for a man who was very immoral and began traveling with him for job-related reasons. He was exposed to pornography while on the road, and he became addicted to it.

He became more and more immoral and so demanding that it was impossible for his wife to satisfy him sexually. The devil had downloaded lies into this man's mind until he became convinced the only way he could find sexual satisfaction was to be immersed in a lifestyle of promiscuous sex.

I tried to talk to him over the phone. I heard the heartbreaking cries of his three young daughters in the background. They were pleading with their daddy not to leave their family.

But he would not listen to them, nor would he listen to me. He insisted his wife did not give him enough sex. I pointed out that a harem could not satisfy a man who is addicted to pornography. He argued about his choice with me, insisting he had found a wonderful lifestyle with his "buddy": The two of them were going to live without moral restraints. He even tried to convince me I should join him in his newfound freedom—a freedom I knew would result in nothing but death and heartache.

This supposed freedom was nothing but a lie straight from the devil.

"How could anyone become so deceived?" you may ask.

It all begins when sin opens the door of the mind and a person invites the devil—and his kingdom of darkness—to step inside. It begins when the weapon of God's Word is laid aside. With each sin, the devil downloads yet more false information into a person's thinking.

The longer a person lingers in an environment of darkness, the more deceived he or she becomes, until truth is twisted into a lie that dominates his or her life.

Once someone has become brainwashed in this way, the devil uses that person as a carrier for sin, in the hopes that he or she will infect others and pull them into defeat. My friend who became infected through his boss is a perfect example of this dynamic. He became infected, so he tried to convince me to participate in his lifestyle of sin as well.

Countering Conspiracy Step #5

Daily we are surrounded by opportunities to listen to the devil's lies. The most effective way to avoid falling prey to wrong thinking is to avoid sin altogether. When the devil tempts us, he is looking for an open door to infect us with his lies. We immediately must slam that door in his face and refuse to step over into sin.

When we do sin, we must keep short accounts with God. Running to God without delay, and never away from Him, should be our method of operation! Condemnation will seek to drive us farther from God, leaving us vulnerable to advanced brainwashing. But we must keep in mind that God is merciful and loving; He is always longing to restore us to right relationship with Him.

We must remember that He gave His only Son to die for our sins, so we would never have to live in darkness and defeat. When we stay in fellowship with our loving heavenly Father, we can stop the devil's conspiracy dead in its tracks.

CHAPTER 15

conspiracy step #6:
distorting a person's concept of god, themselves and others

Few things have a greater impact on our behavior than what we believe. The Bible tells us that as a person "thinks in his heart, so is he" (Prov. 23:7).

What we believe affects how we relate to God and live before Him as individuals, as well as how we treat others. The devil understands that if he can convince us to believe a lie about God, about others and especially about ourselves, it will affect everything we do and say.

As we've discussed, sin opens a door to wrong thinking.

One of the first areas of our thinking to be affected is our self-confidence. Nothing destroys someone's self-confidence more quickly than yielding territory to the devil through sin. This happened to Adam and Eve immediately after they sinned.

God had made them to be rulers of the world. He had commanded them to subdue the earth and have dominion over every living thing (see Gen. 1:28). But after they sinned, Adam and Eve quaked in fear and insecurity.

When God talked to Adam about the incident, Adam did not accept responsibility for his actions but rather replied, "The woman whom You gave to be with me, she gave me of the tree, and I ate" (Gen. 3:12). Notice that Adam shifted the blame to Eve as though he was powerless to resist temptation.

And when God asked Eve about it, she said, "The serpent deceived me, and I ate" (Gen. 3:13). She might as well have said, "The devil made me do it. I am just a helpless victim!"

God had created Adam and Eve in His own image, and the devil did not have the power to make them do anything! They were the ones who had power over the devil. They had the power to do or not to do anything they chose. But sin caused Adam and Eve to see themselves as helpless victims. Instead of exercising authority over the devil, they shifted blame to him as though he had all the power and they had none. This is one way the enemy is able to drag people into darkness.

Sin Distorts the Truth

When people sin, they lose fellowship with God, which changes their self-image. The truth is, we have been created in the image of God to have dominion over, and exercise His righteousness in, the earth. We have been created as God's own children to rule and reign with Jesus throughout eternity.

Sin makes us forget about all that. When the devil convinces us we are victims rather than victors in Christ Jesus, he has gained power to hold us in darkness and control us. Sin also has the power to distort the way we view other people. Adam and Eve were created to have a perfect relationship and live together in harmony, without fear or shame. But after they sinned, they began to hide from and accuse one another.

As a result, when God confronted Adam about his sin, the first thing Adam did was to blame his wife. God had created Eve as a perfect helper for Adam. But after Adam sinned, his concept of Eve became distorted. Instead of appreciating and valuing his wife as a gift from God, Adam saw her as a problem. He indicated something was wrong with "the woman" God had made especially for him. Sin distorted Adam's ideas about Eve and blinded him to the blessing that God had created her to be.

Sin is still working the same way in relationships today. Sin is still convincing men and women there is something "weird" about their spouse. Sin is still causing husbands and wives to forget that God created their spouse to be a perfect partner for them in this life. The devil still is using the same strategy he used against Adam and Eve to divide husbands and wives today.

When we step over into darkness, our perceptions about people change. They may begin to look more like a hindrance than a blessing. Why? Because Satan is an accuser. He is always magnifying the faults of those around us. He wants us to forget that our loved ones have been made in the image of God and that He has a wonderful purpose for every life. Sin gives the devil an open invitation to distort our concept of those around us. If he can do that, he can divide us and rob us of the blessings that come from walking together in unity.

But perhaps the most tragic consequence of sin is not that it distorts our self-image, or even the way we see each other, but rather that it alters our image of God.

Before they sinned, Adam and Eve walked with God in the Garden in the cool of the day. He was their intimate Friend, who was there only to bless and do them good. After they sinned, however, they believed God was harsh and judgmental. They felt that they needed to hide from Him.

The devil knows that if he can distort our image of God, he can succeed in separating us from Him. What we must remember is that nothing we do will ever cause God to stop loving us.

Our God has not changed His nature, and He never will. He is a good God who created everything good to be enjoyed. As our loving Father, He gave His only Son to redeem us to Himself. He is our healer, provider, deliverer and our friend. But if we do not understand that truth in our hearts, we will be afraid of Him—we will hide from the One who is the answer to all of our needs and concerns.

Sin does not change God, but sin does change the image we have of Him. It causes us to view God as an enemy, rather than a friend. The enemy will try to bring in fear and shame in order to separate us from the only One who can set us free from sin!

This is all part of the devil's conspiracy.

He lures us into sin.

He tries to divide us and rob us of the joy we can have in relationships.

He endeavors to separate us from fellowship with God.

The devil wants to convince us we are helpless victims with no power over our own destinies.

He does this by making us forget that we have been created in God's image and that we are His children.

But as believers, we must remember that nothing changes God's love for us—nothing changes His plan for us. He has given us dominion over the devil. Let's assert our authority in Jesus' name—and be victims no more.

Countering Conspiracy Step #6

The best way to counter the devil's distortions is to remind ourselves of what God has said in His Word.

We must remember that we have been created in God's own image, to rule and reign with Jesus for all eternity. We must remember that the person we are married to is God's precious creation. He or she has been made in God's image and created to be our perfect partner in this life. And we must remember that God is a loving Father who wants to bless us and do us only good.

When we know what God has said in His Word and believe it, the devil's lies fall apart.

So, open up God's Word, and find out what He says about *you*.

Read about His great love for you and the plans He has for your life.

Find out what He has to say about your marriage and family.

Then refuse to listen when the devil tells you that God does not love you, your spouse is "weird," your children are hopeless and you are just a helpless victim in life!

No. You are what God says you are, and you can do what God says you can do!

We can counter the devil's conspiracy by abiding in the truth.

When we walk with God and meditate on His Word, the devil will not be able to mess with our thinking. Staying close to the Author of truth and abiding in close fellowship with Him is key to victory over the devil's conspiracy code.

PART IV

the
conspiracy
undone

shameless sexuality

During the time of the so-called Sexual Revolution, a song called "Woodstock" was written that became an anthem of sorts for the ideology of unlimited "freedom" and sexual promiscuity. In hindsight, some of the words to that song are rather startling. The lyrics claim that each of us are "golden" and "stardust" and that we were snared into the "devil's bargain." What we must do, the songwriter declares, is find a way to return to the Garden of Eden.[1]

Along with conveying the idea that we evolved over billions of years, these words send the message that we can somehow redeem ourselves from the "the devil's bargain" that brought shame and fear upon the human race. Of course, we cannot redeem ourselves. Only the spotless blood of God's beloved Son could pay the price for sin, and give us an entrance into fellowship with God.

Still, these words seem to acknowledge that something precious was lost when sin brought the "devil's bargain" into this earth. They express the heart-cry of so many people to "get back to" the beautiful world that existed before sin brought fear, shame and corruption into the earth.

Sadly, the message of the Sexual Revolution was the same message the devil had whispered to Adam and Eve in the Garden: that God and His laws were standing between people and true sexual fulfillment. This message from the enemy asserted that the way for people to experience freedom was to throw off the "shackles" of God's morality and live for their own selfish desires.

As was the case with Adam and Eve, this thinking did not lead anyone "back to the Garden." It did not result in the freedom, beauty or fulfillment the devil had promised. Like all sin, it led only to devastation and death. We clearly see the results of that deception and destruction in our culture today.

It is true that God created sex as a beautiful gift to bring joy and pleasure to His people and to fulfill His purposes in the earth. Even sinners seem to understand that sex is intended to be something wonderful as they struggle in their own fallen way to find the path "back" to sex as God intended it to be. It is heartbreaking to consider how, through sin and deception, the devil has used that inner longing to drive people farther and farther away from God's plan.

The good news is this: There is a way "back to the Garden" for those who know God and are redeemed through the blood of His Son. When Jesus Christ paid the price for our sins, He redeemed us and made a way for us to get back to the covenant of blessing and peace that God originally planned for us. When we walk with God and understand His principles, we can live the way that He originally designed us to live: free from fear and shame. Fulfilled in our sexuality.

I call this way of living "shameless sexuality."

When we live in shameless sexuality, we experience sex the way God intended. A lifestyle of shameless sexuality is a lifestyle of victory, free from bondage, torment and fear. It is possible for us to live this way, even in the midst of a very fallen world. We can abstain from sex until married, and then we can experience sex in marriage as the paradise of joy and fulfillment God designed it to be.

There is no denying the world is very dark. We are surrounded by the results of the Fall, and temptations bombard us from every side. But we can live above the ways of this world. We can live in God's purposes and love as He intended.

How?

By incorporating the following six simple principles into our lives. Taking these practical steps will help us avoid temptation and live victoriously in the area of sex.

Note

 1. Joni Mitchell, "Woodstock," © 1969 Crazy Crow Music, Sony/ATV Tunes LLC.

victory step #1:
having a scriptural worldview of sex

You have a worldview, whether you know it or not. Your view is the "lens" through which you see the world around you. It affects your perceptions, and therefore, your reactions to everything you encounter in life.

Two people may look at the same thing but see it differently because they are seeing it through different "lenses." People from every faith—Christians, Hindus, Muslims, atheists, and so on—have a certain view of reality that guides their decisions, and ultimately their destinies.

As believers, our worldview is scriptural. That means we see everything through the "lens" of God's Word. The Bible is our point of reference in making decisions. At one time, it could have been said that a scriptural worldview was the prevailing view in our culture. That, however, is no longer the case. We are now living in a postmodern world, which denies the existence of God and rejects the Bible.

Secular Humanism

Another worldview, called "secular humanism," has become a driving force in our society. Secular humanism is an evolution-based, man-centered perspective that attributes all of our behavior to our godless nature. According to this worldview, there is no God, and therefore there is no such thing as absolute truth. By believing that everything has evolved, there is no right or wrong—only the law of "survival of the fittest." The manifesto of secular humanism says, "There is no God, so we must save ourselves."

This humanistic worldview has infected our society. It is influencing our schools, our government, our entertainment and even our churches. Without a moral compass to help us discern right from wrong, our world is sliding rapidly into a state of corruption and despair.

In our postmodern world, we cannot assume that people—even those who attend church—have a Christian worldview. Many liberal churches teach secular humanism rather than biblical truth. Some Christians are more influenced by secular humanism than by the Bible, especially in their attitudes about sex. Because of this, sin and failure creep into their lives.

Once we reject the idea of God as our Creator, we lose our understanding of His principles and the moral absolutes that hold the universe together. If we accept the belief that people are the random product of lightning striking a slime pool somewhere in the distant past, that belief will affect our perception of reality. In that reality, there is no moral basis to order our thinking, so "caveman rules" are as good as any others. There is no such thing as "right" or "wrong," so why have any limits on behavior?

"Eat, drink and be merry, for tomorrow we may die" (Eccles. 8:15).

The Slippery Slope to Depravity

This concept may appear harmless to many people, but in reality, that thinking leads to a chaotic world. Once a society has accepted that "there is no right or wrong," it does not take long to slide down the slippery slope into total moral depravity.

Disturbing evidence of this in our society is the growing acceptance of pedophilia. There is an organization in America today that exists for the sole purpose of promoting and legalizing sex between adults and children. It is called the North American Man-Boy Love Association. Rather than being prosecuted for advocating child abuse, this organization is assisted by well-funded advocacy groups. To any normal human being, the very idea is crazy, but secular humanists do not think the way we do. In their minds, there is no right or wrong. Everything is up for discussion.

Nonsacred Marriage

Another outcome of the humanist mindset is the idea that marriage is a social custom that has "evolved" for the sake of convenience. Since humanists believe there is no God, they see nothing sacred about marriage, sexuality or anything else for that matter. Instead of considering marriage to be a lifelong covenant, they view marriage as a legal arrangement, to be made or dissolved at the whims of those involved.

Secular humanism has also fostered the idea that it is impossible for men to be monogamous. This view is based on the belief that men "evolved" to spread their seed, so it is normal for a man to be immoral and cheat on his wife. A woman is supposed to accept that idea and never expect her husband to be faithful to her or to his marriage vows.

The Nutty Professors

Secular humanism has affected every institution in our society, but perhaps none more than the educational system. Liberal, humanistic teaching now dominates most institutions of higher learning. Many professors do not believe in God, truth or moral absolutes.

Some sociologists are teaching very bizarre ideas about marriage and sex. Take this one: Humankind has "evolved" to such a degree that we now have the *need* to change marriage partners every seven years. I'm sure you've heard of the "Seven-Year Itch." This philosophy says, "If you are tired of your spouse, you can trade her or him in for a new one every seven years. You have evolved to be that way; and if you try to stay in an unhappy marriage, you are fighting against nature."

How can you build a life with a person who is not going to be around for very long?

The answer is: *You don't.*

Married couples that subscribe to this way of thinking have no security, no intimacy and no hope for the future—they simply cannot build a stable life together. Without a committed, lifelong relationship, people live in constant fear, because certain heartache is just around the corner.

The world of secular humanism is a world without God—and a world without God is not a safe place for anyone.

The Biblical Description of Humanists

The apostle Paul seemed to know all about this humanistic mindset that has invaded our culture. In his letter to Timothy, he talked about the future:

> But know this, that in the last days perilous times will come. For men will be lovers of themselves, lovers of money, boasters, proud, blasphemers, disobedient to parents, unthankful, unholy, unloving, unforgiving, slanderers, without self-control, brutal, despisers of good, traitors, headstrong, haughty, lovers of pleasure rather than lovers of God, having a form of godliness but denying its power. And from such people turn away! (2 Tim. 3:1-5).

The last days will be perilous times, Paul says, because of the way humankind will think and act. He tells us that in the future men and woman will be . . .

"Lovers of themselves." What an apt description of people today! It seems our society is totally self-absorbed. Most people show little consideration for others and certainly have no willingness to makes sacrifices for the good of others. This makes the times in which we live "perilous."

"Lovers of money." Our generation has more material comforts than any other in the history of humankind. Yet we seem to be obsessed with obtaining more and more "stuff."

Money in itself has become the driving force in most lives, along with the dream of obtaining lavish wealth. There is a television program called *I Want to Be a Hilton*, which caters to those who want to be as rich as Paris Hilton. Is she an outstanding role model? Does she have integrity or upstanding character?

No. Quite the opposite.

Simply because of her wealth, people want to be like her—especially young people. They mistakenly think that having material wealth will make them happy and solve all their problems. Talk about a deception!

"Blasphemers." A blasphemer is someone who says things that are against God and against what is holy. And our nation is full of such people. Blasphemy is commonplace and considered by many to be "funny."

What perilous times we live in!

"Disobedient to parents." More and more children are becoming rebellious toward the authority of their parents. Fewer and fewer parents honor God, so of course, parents do have something to do with the fact that their children refuse to honor and respect them as God has commanded. It's heartbreaking to hear how some children brutalize their parents, and others even go so far as to kill them. That is a breakdown of God's order and a sign of very perilous times.

"Unloving." The word "unloving" in this verse becomes more interesting when you examine its meaning in the original Greek. There are five different words for "love" in the Greek language. And one of these words is *storge*. *Storge* signifies the natural love that occurs in a family, such as the love of a mother for her child. Yet the word "unloving" in this verse is the word *astorgos*—meaning that *storge* love is missing. It means "without natural affection" or "hardhearted toward kindred"—and it signifies that the normal love of a family is not present.

This lack of natural family bonding is clearly evident in our society. Only 20 years ago, it was extremely rare to hear of a mother abandoning her children. Often, we would hear of a man abandoning his wife and children, but we almost never heard of a woman leaving her children and wanting nothing more to do with them.

That is no longer the case. Today, it is as common for a woman to abandon her family as it is for a man.

It has also become more and more common for parents to victimize their children sexually. This activity is abnormal and strictly forbidden in the Bible. A natural, loving bond between parent and child excludes even the consideration of such a violation. Unfortunately, to a certain extent in our society, natural family love and affection have been eroded, and more unnatural, abusive behavior has resulted.

This "unloving" atmosphere makes the times in which we live perilous.

"Without self-control." So many people in our society have little or no self-control.

Date rape is a horrible example of this fact. It's hard to believe this is epidemic on college campuses. So many young men of this generation simply have not been disciplined by their parents. They have learned from an early age that they can have whatever they want, even if it means violating others in the process.

These young men also have learned how to control their parents, and their environment as well. They don't take no for an answer. Never have they been taught to restrain their appetites. They do not understand delayed gratification, discipline or sacrifice.

Such young people are "without self-control"—and they make the world a perilous place.

"Despisers of good." Why, you may ask, would anyone despise something good? Take marriage for instance. The Bible tells us that God instituted marriage between a man and a woman. Yet the word "marriage," as it is traditionally understood, is despised by certain groups in

our country. People who live together abhor the word, while many homosexual activists seek to redefine it.

When something *good* like marriage is despised, we are living in perilous times.

"Lovers of pleasure rather than lovers of God." Many people who believe in God, and even claim to love God, choose pleasure over obedience to His Word. In doing this, they give pleasure the place that God should have in their lives. Pleasure rules their decisions, rather than righteousness. When pleasure rules, rather than God and His laws, we are in perilous times.

"Having a form of godliness but denying its power. And from such people turn away." When Paul warns that some people will have "a form of godliness," he means that they will seem to be godly in certain ways. Even though their outward "form" looks godly, they deny the "power" that goes with true godliness.

The word translated as "power" here is the Greek word *dunamis*. It is the same word Jesus used to describe the power of the Holy Spirit that would come on the day of Pentecost. He said to the disciples, "You shall receive power when the Holy Spirit has come upon you" (Acts 1:8).

Many Christian people are aware of this meaning of the word *dunamis* when used in the context of spiritual power that works signs, wonders and miracles. They may not be aware that the word has another meaning, one that signifies *moral power* and *excellence*.

So here Paul is warning us about people who have an outward form of godliness, but who deny the *morality* of godliness. These people deny the moral authority of God's Word, which gives power and excellence to true godliness. Many people around us deny the power of true godliness.

One enormously popular and gifted talk-show celebrity is a prominent example. She has become a spiritual counselor to millions of women because she openly confesses Christ *and* emphasizes the importance of "spirituality." However, for years this celebrity has lived with a man to whom she is not married. She also endorses homosexuality as a lifestyle. In other words, she has a form of godliness, but she denies the moral authority set forth by God in the Bible. She talks about praying to God, but the "god" she prays to is a god without morality. That sort of "faith" has no power behind it, because the moral power and excellence of God has already been denied.

Yet this kind of "religion" is compatible with secular humanism. Secular humanism does not always reject God. It will tolerate the idea of God *as long as there is no obligation to God's moral authority.*

Why?

Because people are "lovers of pleasure rather than lovers of God." They are willing to believe in God, as long as it does not interfere with their selfish desires.

As believers, we have a moral obligation to live according to the truth God has set forth in His Word. If you believe in Jesus Christ and the Bible, you cannot also embrace homosexuality, sex outside of marriage or any other type of immorality. To do so is to deny the moral power and excellence of your faith.

A Scriptural Worldview

As believers in Jesus Christ, our worldview begins and ends with what God has said in the Bible. A scriptural worldview about sex and morality is laid out very clearly for us in the book of 1 Corinthians:

> Do you not know that the unrighteous will not inherit the kingdom of God? Do not be deceived. Neither fornicators, nor idolaters, nor adulterers, nor homosexuals, nor sodomites, nor thieves, nor covetous, nor drunkards, nor revilers, nor extortioners will inherit the kingdom of God. And such were some of you. But you were washed, but you were sanctified, but you were jus-

tified in the name of the Lord Jesus and by the Spirit of our God. All things are lawful for me, but all things are not helpful. All things are lawful for me, but I will not be brought under the power of any. Foods for the stomach and the stomach for foods, but God will destroy both it and them. Now the body is not for sexual immorality but for the Lord, and the Lord for the body. And God both raised up the Lord and will also raise us up by His power. Do you not know that your bodies are members of Christ? Shall I then take the members of Christ and make them members of a harlot? Certainly not! Or do you not know that he who is joined to a harlot is one body with her? For "The two," He says, "shall become one flesh." But he who is joined to the Lord is one Spirit with Him. Flee sexual immorality. Every sin that a man does is outside the body, but he who commits sexual immorality sins against his own body. Or do you not know that your body is the temple of the Holy Spirit who is in you, whom you have from God, and you are not your own? You were bought at a price; therefore glorify God in your body and in your spirit, which are God's (6:9–20).

The worldview of secular humanism tells us there is nothing wrong with fornication, cohabitation or homosexuality. It says the bonds of marriage are manmade and can therefore be broken at will or by whim.

If you believe there is nothing wrong with these beliefs, the Bible says you have been very deceived.

If you practice these sins without repentance, the Bible makes it clear that you will not inherit the kingdom of God.

The world shoves its immoral view of sex down our throats.

The Word of God tells us something very different—it tells us our bodies do not belong to us, but to God. Our bodies are temples of the Holy Spirit. We do not have the right to use them any way we see fit.

Sex is not a hollow or meaningless act, but rather a wonderful gift God has reserved for marriage. We have a responsibility to honor that gift, and keep it holy.

Scriptural or Secular?

How can we know the difference between God's ideas about sex and those of the world? The best way to discern the difference is to investigate God's ideas about love versus the world's ideas.

Secular humanism acknowledges a type of "love" that is vastly different from God's kind of love. The "love" of secular humanism is a love for this world and for the things that are in this world. The Bible tells us to stay away from that kind of love:

> Do not love the world or the things in the world. If anyone loves the world, the love of the Father is not in him. For all that is in the world—the lust of the flesh, the lust of the eyes, and the pride of life—is not of the Father but is of the world. And the world is passing away, and the lust of it; but he who does the will of God abides forever (1 John 2:15-17).

The difference between the world's view of sex and God's view of sex is really the difference between their views of love.

This Scripture says that what the world calls "love" is actually "the lust of the flesh, the lust of the eye and the boastful pride of life."

What the world calls "love" is really just *lust*.

According to this Scripture, anyone who loves in that way does not have "the love of the Father" in him or her. If a person is full of lust, that person is not full of the love of God.

Lust has three elements to it: Lust is *immediate*, it is *illicit*, and it is *"I" centered.*

1. *Lust wants immediate gratification.* In other words, it wants what it wants, and it wants it *right now*. Lust is never willing to wait until the time is right, or until it is best for someone else. It is not willing to delay its own gratification until marriage or to seriously consider the consequences of its actions. Lust is a driving force, and it demands its own way in the moment, with no thought for the future.

2. *Lust is illicit.* Those who are guided by lust are willing to break any rule to get what they want. They do not care what the law says. They do not care what the Bible says. They do not care what anyone else says. They have a desire, and they are willing to cross any line to get that desire satisfied.

3. *Lust is "I" centered.* For people driven by lust, the world revolves around "me, myself and I." As long as their needs are met, they are unconcerned about the needs of others or the consequences of their actions. They are blind to the pain and suffering they are causing.

Love that is immediate, illicit, and "I" centered is not love at all—it is lust. And lust brings nothing but chaos, hurt and emptiness.

God's love is a very different thing. God's love is sacrificial, scriptural, selfless.

The love of God is willing to sacrifice for others. People who are walking in the love of God do not demand their own rights or insist that their own needs be met. They are willing to set aside their desires and delay gratification for the good of others. This is the "God kind" of love. This is the love God demonstrated when He sacrificed what was most precious to Him: His only begotten Son.

Because God loved us, He gave His beloved Son, who had never done anything worthy of punishment, to suffer and die for our sins. That is sacrifice. That is the love of God. And that makes the Cross the greatest symbol of love in the history of the universe.

God's love is scriptural. While lust is illicit, the love of God is willing to live within the confines of God's Word and to abide by the rules set forth in it.

Love is always concerned about the other person; therefore, love thinks about the consequences of sin. Love says, "I am not going to cross this line, because if I do, I know that it will lead to unhappiness and destruction. And I do not want that for you or for our relationship."

The "God kind" of love is willing to be ruled by God's Word, rather than by the demands of the flesh.

The "God kind" of love is selfless. It lives for God first, then for others. People who walk in God's love are more concerned about the needs of their spouse than their own needs. They are not consumed with what they want, but with what God wants. When it comes to sex, they refrain from doing anything that is not good for their partner, because they are there to serve and give, not to take and make demands.

Great sex does not come from knowing a certain "technique" but rather from both spouses serving each other unselfishly. Two selfish people who think only of their own needs cannot have good sex. Selfishness makes sex frustrating and unfulfilling, but the selfless love of God makes sex wonderful.

Lust Versus Love

It has been said, "Love can always wait to give, but lust can never wait to get." This is a good way to measure your attitude toward sex. If your attitude toward sex is selfish and demanding, you are walking in lust, not love. But if your approach to sex is selfless and scriptural, you are walking in the love of God.

Our worldview is the "lens" that determines our view of love and sex. A worldview driven by lust leads to insecurity, frustration and bondage. But a worldview ruled by the love of God results in sex that is safe, joyous and fulfilling.

Although the world is always showing us sex through the lens of secular humanism, it is possible to look at sex through a different lens. We can look at sex through the lens of God's Word and allow His love to rule our lives.

If we do this, we will live in shameless sexuality, free from the Fig Leaf Conspiracy.

victory step #2:
obtaining wisdom

Jesus' disciples listened to His teaching for a long time and soaked in a lot of His wisdom. They witnessed His miracles and saw how He lived a sinless life. When Jesus sent them out to minister, He warned them they would have to be *wise* in order to succeed. He compared the world to a pack of ravenous wolves, just waiting to devour them: "Behold, I send you out as sheep in the midst of wolves. Therefore be wise as serpents and harmless as doves" (Matt. 10:16).

If Jesus' disciples had to be wise in their day, we are going to have to be wiser still in ours.

Every time we step out the door or turn on the television set, we step out into a world of temptation waiting to devour us. When we send our children to school or the mall, they are like innocent sheep going into the midst of wolves. Sin surrounds us on every side, and the devil is ready to devour anyone who is foolish enough to give into his temptations.

The apostle Paul revealed that evil days require believers to take careful steps. He said, "See then that you walk circumspectly, not as fools but as wise, redeeming the time, because the days are evil" (Eph. 5:15–16).

No question—we are living in evil days. In order to live a life of shameless sexuality, we must walk "circumspectly"—which means we must use the wisdom of God to keep ourselves safe from the devil's attacks. If we have children, we must use God's wisdom to keep our children safe.

Ten Standards for Parental Wisdom

There are practical standards we can implement to help us in our personal lives and to help us as parents. Let's begin with wisdom for parents.

1. Be a Good Role Model

No person or thing has a greater influence in a child's life during his or her formative years than that child's parents.

The Bible says, "Train up a child in the way he should go, and when he is old, he will not depart from it" (Prov. 22:6). As parents, we have a responsibility to train our children so that they can succeed in life. Much of the "training" we do is through our conduct and attitudes. It has been said that what our children learn from us is more "caught" than taught.

Your children will "catch" your attitudes about sex, your language about sex and the way that you handle your own sexuality as a married couple. Whether or not you are aware of it, your children are watching you. If you want them to live in shameless sexuality, you will have to live your life that way as well.

Sad to say, 70 percent of all pornography eventually finds its way into the hands of minors. What is even sadder still is the fact that many young people get their first taste of sex from some sort of entertainment or magazine a parent has left lying around the house. This sets these children up to have a very fallen view of sex from the very beginning.

We had a heartbreaking experience one day when we went to look at a home that was "For Sale by Owner." We started touring the house and found this home was filled with all sorts of pornographic material. In every room there were erotic statues, pornographic magazines in open view and sexual paraphernalia strewn about.

When we walked into one of the back rooms, we met two eleven-year-old girls, at least one of whom lived in that house. Our hearts ached as we realized what these innocent little girls were exposed to in their own home every day. What chance did they have to grow into adults who would have a healthy view of sexuality? Their parents had robbed them of their innocence. In doing so, they had robbed them of the opportunity to understand sex as the shameless and beautiful gift that God created it to be.

If we are ashamed of sex, our children will be ashamed of it.

If we approach it from the world's view of lust and shame, our children will develop that same attitude.

As parents, we must live before our children in such a way that they can see the goodness of God and understand God's attitudes toward sex, rather than those of the world.

2. Proactively Discuss Sex with Your Children—Make It an Open Subject

The devil tries to keep the issue of sex in darkness so that he can be your children's sex educator. Parents must take the fig leaves off the subject and make sex an open topic in the home. It is important for parents to let their children know there is no shame in talking about sex, and it's important for parents to take the initiative in discussing it.

Nowadays, children are getting sexual information earlier than ever before. So, it is a good idea for parents to start talking about sex when their children are around the age of eight or nine, before they enter puberty.

Parents should talk to them about their body parts, what those parts are for, the correct names for those parts, and other such basics.

Parents should also talk to them about masturbation and other temptations, and help prepare them to deal with various situations they may encounter.

It is very important for children to know that sex is up for discussion and that they can talk to their parents about it at any time. When parents bring the subject of sex out into the light, it helps their children develop an attitude of shameless sexuality.

3. Set Parameters for Entertainment

No parent would leave his or her child in a room full of wolves and expect that child to guard himself. No reasonable parent would leave his or her child in a room full of candy and expect that child to restrain his or her appetite. In the same way, children need to be protected more than ever from wrong entertainment. God has placed parents in their children's lives precisely to guide and protect them.

If you are like me, you have probably noticed that children these days are electronic geniuses. Our granddaughters are three years old, and they already know how to work our televisions and DVD player (for all I know, they may be able to hack into our computer as well!). With just the click of a button, children can access a virtual "candy store" of sexual temptation at any time of the day, on just about any channel of the television. Many television programs and even commercials are full of sexually explicit material. Much of the music today has lyrics that are sexually explicit or full of violence and hate.

It is simply not wise to assume that children will have the maturity or discernment to turn the channel to watch something more appropriate—or listen to something more wholesome. Children need their parents to watch out for them, protect them *and* hold them accountable for what they listen to on the radio and watch on TV.

The bottom line is that parents need to monitor every form of media that comes into their home. If children are going to see a movie, parents should make it their business to find out the content of that movie. If children are going to use the Internet, it should be out in the open, not in their room where there is no accountability for what they are viewing. There is just too much questionable material out there, not to mention online predators, who would love to talk to your children!

4. Carefully Monitor Your Children's Friends and Their Activities
Most parents make every effort to raise their children to be good people. But those efforts can be undone by time spent in bad company. The Bible tells us, "Do not be deceived. 'Evil company corrupts good habits'" (1 Cor. 15:33).

You can raise the best children in the world, but if you allow them to be around bad company, their good habits will eventually be corrupted. This is just the truth. You absolutely must monitor who your children's friends are—who they are hanging out with. Though we are not to be snobs, we have a responsibility to guard and protect our children and raise them in the right way.

The Bible says that "evil company" is a corrupting influence. When our children were growing up, Karen and I would notice a definite difference in them after they had spent time with certain children. For this reason, we were very careful about not allowing them to play with those kids. We were very willing to "import" children from across town rather than have our children spend time with kids in the neighborhood who were not a good influence.

Now, perhaps more than ever, parents must be vigilant.

No child is perfect, including my own. But it would be shortsighted to send your child into a home where *Playboy* magazines are lying around or unacceptable movies are being viewed or profanity is being used. It is not helpful for a child to be around people whose values conflict with what he or she is taught at home—that only leads to confusion and, eventually, corruption.

Karen and I did not expect our children's friends to be perfect. But as much as possible, we wanted to make sure the atmosphere of the homes in which our kids would spend time was pure and clean. We wanted to know that those parents shared our values and moral parameters. We knew that if their rules in the home were the same as ours, it would eliminate a great deal of confusion and temptation for our children. When you protect the spiritual atmosphere around your children, you are protecting them from the corruption and shame the devil tries to introduce into their thinking. Guarding their hearts and minds by monitoring the company they keep is part of helping your children develop a mindset of shameless sexuality.

5. Help Your Children "Premake" Sexual Decisions

"Premade" decisions are powerful. When you have decided beforehand that you will not succumb to sexual temptation, you have gained an advantage. Here's why: Having already thought through a situation and developed a strategy, you are much less likely to react based on the pressures of the moment.

That is one reason Karen and I made it a priority to sit down with our children and openly discuss situations that they might encounter. We asked them questions such as:

- "What are you going to do if you are with a group of kids, and they start to pass around a racy magazine?"

- "What are you going to do if you are at a party and some kids start to go into rooms and make out—and you are being pressured to do the same thing?"

- "What are you going to do if you are on a date and your date starts to pressure you sexually?"

It is very helpful to talk through these situations ahead of time and help your children think about how to handle each one. When they have already thought it through and made decisions about how to respond, they will be prepared for the devil's attacks. Premaking decisions is a very powerful way for children to avoid sexual sin and live a life of shameless sexuality.

6. Make Church a High Priority in Your Children's Lives

How busy are you? If you are like most parents, you are extremely busy! Schoolwork, sports, ballet lessons, carpools, chores and just the daily business of living—all of these activities compete for the limited time of families. Of all the demands that press on parents and kids, none is more important than making sure that your children get to church.

There is no sport, no activity and no academic accomplishment that can take the place of the power available in Christian fellowship. No excuse is good enough to justify forsaking that vital part of a victorious life. In his letter to the Hebrews, Paul talked about how important church attendance is:

> Let us consider one another in order to stir up love and good works, not forsaking the assembling of ourselves together, as is the manner of some, but exhorting one another, and so much the more as you see the Day approaching (Heb. 10:24-25).

The "Day" that Paul is talking about is the end of this age and the coming of Jesus Christ. As that Day approaches, Paul says we will need Christian fellowship more than ever before. More than ever before we will need to exhort one another, encourage one another and stir one another up to live for God.

There can be little doubt that we are living in that "Day." Every time we step outside the walls of the church, we are bombarded with negative peer pressure, rebellion and immorality. If we are going to survive in this world of sin, we need the love and support of other believers.

And if adults need the strength that comes from Christian fellowship, children need it even more. We cannot expect them to survive the attacks of the enemy if they are isolated and alone.

This is why Karen and I had a firm rule that our children had to be in church, regardless of what else was going on in their lives. We were not legalistic about it, and we allowed them to have fun. At the same time, there was no excuse for missing church—no homework assignment or sporting event was more important than attending church.

Children need to hear the Word of God preached, just as we do. Our children need a refuge from the voices of the world, just as we do.

I realize that church kids are not perfect, and that some of the socializing that goes on in a youth group may be far from ideal. Still, the focus of that group is God, and that alone can make a huge difference in a child's life. Because children spend so much of their time tied up with worldly concerns and cares, they need to be involved consistently in a group that has God, not sports or school or the latest fad, as its focus.

So, make a commitment today to keep your kids in church. Having Christian fellowship helps counteract the voices of the world and encourages your children to lead a life of shameless sexuality.

7. Regulate and Discuss Expectations for Dating

In our home, we set strict parameters for dating. For starters, our children couldn't date until they were age 16. They could have friends of the opposite sex, but that was it. Even after they turned 16, we regulated their dating very strictly. I believe this is every parent's responsibility.

Children and teenagers alike will either live up or down to parents' expectations. It is important for parents to let their teenagers know exactly what expectations they have.

For example, we let our children know we expected them *not* to French kiss. We expected them to avoid any situation in which they might be alone with a date and physical contact could occur. We let them know that their virginity was precious—and we expected them to keep that sacred, reserved only for their future spouse.

This is just practical wisdom. Without predetermined standards, one thing can lead to another. Then before either person knows what has happened, they have fallen into sin.

A recent study found that if two people spend a cumulative 90 hours alone together, kissing and embracing, they will inevitably have sexual intercourse. When you think about it, 90 hours is not a very long time in a dating situation, and things can progress quickly if nature is just allowed to "take its course." It's really not surprising: If two people are alone somewhere, lying down next to each other, French kissing and having a lot of physical contact, it is only a matter of time before they will have intercourse.

In my years as a pre-marriage counselor, I have heard this story repeated time and again—and it happens to the best of people.

It is wise to set parameters ahead of time, and then stick to those parameters. I believe the best thing a couple can do is to avoid kissing altogether until they are married. While some people may think that is a puritanical idea, it is a very effective way to avoid temptation and sin.

Not everyone will set that standard, I realize, but everyone should set a standard high enough to protect both people from temptation. For example, a couple may agree that they will kiss, but they will not French kiss. They may agree to hold hands, but not to hug each other. Or my personal favorite: A teenage couple agrees that they can be a bit more affectionate in a room with their parents present, feet on the floor and Pastor Jimmy staring sternly at them from the TV!

When our children started dating, we set very strict time limits about when they needed to be home. We also scrutinized the people they dated—we didn't allow them to date just anyone. If we did not trust someone, our children were not allowed to date that person.

At one time, our daughter Julie had a boyfriend we loved, but then she broke up with him. Of course she had a right to make that choice. We then heard through the grapevine she was planning on going with another boy, and we became concerned because we knew this boy had a reputation and he lived up to it. He was not someone we trusted.

So I had this little exchange with Julie about it:

"Julie, I heard that you broke up with so-and-so."

"Yes, that's right."

"Well, that's your own business, of course. But I also heard something else. I heard that you were going to go out with so-and-so. Is that right?"

"Yeah, he asked me out."

"Over my dead body, Julie. You will never go out with that boy. Do you understand me? If I find out that you have talked to him on the phone or spent time with him, I promise you there will be serious repercussions. You got that?"

"Daaaaad!" she wailed.

Julie was very exasperated with me. But it didn't matter.

"Julie, that's the way it is."

Interestingly enough, within five minutes she was back with her old boyfriend.

Parents have a responsibility to set ground rules for how, when and who their children date. Parents are to protect their children, as much as possible, from unhealthy relationships.

Young girls especially need to be protected, and that is a daddy's job. I believe it is the responsibility of every father to give dirty looks to the boys who come to date their daughters. This came quite naturally to me, and I would expect every father worth his salt to do the same. It doesn't matter whether you like the young man or not. As dads, our job is to put the fear of God in those young men, and keep it there.

When my daughter had her first date, I actually liked the young man. But that didn't stop me from glaring at him when he arrived and giving him the "Terminator" look!

One of my favorite "Dad the Terminator" stories is about a man who had a unique method of letting boys know they had to answer to him for how they treated his daughter. This dad told his daughter he wanted to talk to her date when he arrived.

She was afraid her dad was going to scare her date off, and she begged, "Dad, please be nice to him." Her dad reassured her that he would be nice and that he just wanted a few words with the boy before they left to go out. So when the young man arrived, the girl sent him into her dad's study, explaining that her dad just wanted a few words with him.

The girl's father asked the young man to be seated, and then he took out a baseball bat and showed it to him. On that baseball bat were written all the rules that man had for dating his daughter. He began to read the rules, one by one.

1. You will respect my daughter, and you will not touch her in a sexual way.

2. You will have her home on time. And "on time" is when I say it is.

The father continued to read all the rules written on the bat until he had finished. Then he stood up and asked the young man, "Do you understand?"

And the young man said, "Yes, sir."

Then the father replied, "All right then, you can date my daughter."

The boy and the man's daughter went on their date that night, and the young man had her home on time. But that is not the end of the story.

The next week the young man came to date the girl again, and he asked if he could talk to her father before they left to go out. She sent him into her dad's study, and once again the father asked the young man to be seated.

Then the young man said, "Sir, there is something I would like to ask you."

"Yes, what is it?" the father replied.

"Well," the young man said, "my sister has a date tomorrow night, and my dad was just wondering . . . Can he borrow your bat?"

It's a humorous story, but one that also has something important to say—namely, that we need to be very protective of our children as they enter the dating scene. Remember, as parents, we would never put them behind the wheel of a car without preparing them to deal with issues they will face on busy, dangerous streets. In the same way, we must not send our children out into the world without preparing them for dating and helping them avoid the pitfalls that can so easily arise.

By having high standards and a system of accountability in your home, your children can enjoy dating in a safe atmosphere and build habits that will result in a life of shameless sexuality.

8. Prepare Your Children for Marriage and Remove Their Fears

We sent a cameraman out to a local high school to interview students about marriage for a segment on our *MarriageToday* television program. He came back to the studio with sobering findings. He said, "Every child I talked to is terrified of marriage."

Terrified of marriage? Why would anyone be terrified of marriage? Marriage as God designed it is a wonderful thing.

Sadly, many children today have not seen positive, successful marriages, and as a result many are terrified to marry. Because of that, people are waiting longer than ever to marry. Right now, the average age of marriage for men is about 28, and 25 for women. At the same time, children are entering puberty earlier than ever before. These two things taken together have created a promiscuity problem.

Since sex is reserved for a lifelong covenant relationship, marriage is the only place where young people can express their sexuality in a legitimate way. However, many people are remaining single throughout their prime sexual years simply because they are so afraid of being married.

Of course, there is an age in which children are too young and immature to marry, such as 15 or 16 years old. But I do not believe there is anything harmful about marrying at age 19 or 20, as long as the couple is adequately prepared. (Karen and I married at age 19, and I am very glad about it. Even though it was tough sledding at first, it was the best thing for me—and probably kept me out of jail!)

As parents, it is our job to educate and prepare our children for marriage. Not all 19-year-olds are too immature or financially inept to handle the responsibilities of marriage. The issue is not age, but rather the issue is preparedness.

Parents can do a lot to prepare their children for marriage and calm their fears. Let your kids know how great marriage is. Tell them they can succeed at it. Give them practical information to help them understand how to be married successfully by following God's plan. Some parents try to influence their children to delay marriage until every detail of their life is in perfect order. I do not believe this is healthy. Why? Since marriage is the only place where sexuality can be legitimately expressed, having our children wait until they are 25 or 30 to get married could just set them up for sexual immorality and the heartache it brings.

The apostle Paul understood God's attitude about this. He said, "It is better to marry than to burn with passion" (1 Cor. 7:9). Young people have a lot of sexual passion, and God created marriage as the place for that passion to be expressed.

So consider starting today to prepare your children for marriage. Allay their fears about marriage and give them the information they need to find a suitable spouse and build a successful marriage.

When young adults are prepared for marriage and unafraid of its challenges, they can look forward to expressing their sexuality in a shameless way, according to God's plans and purposes.

9. Monitor How Your Children Dress

It is very important to monitor how your children dress. Why? If you allow your children to dress in a sexually provocative way, they will begin to act in a sexually provocative way.

Think about it this way: When someone drops a hook into the water, he or she is usually hoping to catch something. If you allow your children to walk around with "bait" written all over their clothing, it is only a matter of time before "fish" grab it.

It is possible to be fashionable and modest at the same time, although that may be difficult to believe, judging from today's popular fashions. Young girls are wearing pants that are too low and too tight, and tops that are too low or almost nonexistent. Young men walk around with their underwear showing, and their pants hanging so low that I want to pull their belt loops up into their armpits!

But it's not really the boys that I'm terribly concerned about. It's the girls. Young women can be naïve about the effect immodest clothing can have on young boys. Since boys are very visual, if they see girls wearing sexy clothing, then they will think about sex! It is our job as parents to teach our daughters about this particular "fact of life" and to help them have high standards of modesty. We must help our daughters understand that sleazy fashions take away from their beauty and preciousness, and open them up to the wrong kind of attention from the opposite sex.

To this end, we should also go shopping with our children—boys and girls alike—and approve of the clothing before allowing them to buy it. If an outfit is immodest, we must not allow our child to have it, even if the child wants to buy it with his or her own money.

As parents we also need to check out what our kids are wearing before they go out the door to school or to meet friends. If our children are wearing something that is too revealing, we need to ask our kids to change into something more appropriate.

We have a responsibility as parents to teach our children to dress modestly, and then insist they do it. This is one more standard we as parents can implement to help our children live in shameless sexuality.

10. Pray for Your Children's Sexual Protection

Use spiritual warfare to fight for and protect your children. Remember, the power of prayer is a parent's greatest tool.

While we must, of course, use wisdom in the natural realm, we must also know there is a spiritual realm in which angels and demons operate. Some of those demonic spirits are after our children. As parents, it is our job to declare our authority over demonic attacks and wage spiritual warfare on behalf of our children.

Paul talked about this war we fight in the spirit realm: "For though we walk in the flesh, we do not war according to the flesh. For the weapons of our warfare are not carnal but mighty in God" (2 Cor. 10:3–4). God has given us mighty, effectual spiritual weapons. It is impossible for us to watch over our children every minute of every day, but we can call on angels to protect them at all times. We can and should use our spiritual weapons to keep the devil away from our children.

When our children were growing up, Karen and I constantly prayed for them in this way:

Lord, send mighty warring angels to protect our children. Make them invisible to every sexual predator, and protect them from anyone with evil desires. We bind every demon of lust. We bind every demon of deception. We bind every demon of immorality. We bind every demon that would come to steal, kill or destroy our children, in Jesus' name.

The Bible says, "The effective, fervent prayer of a righteous man avails much" (Jas. 5:16). We prayed fervently for our children, and

God protected them. Like all kids, ours had challenges. But our prayers kept them safe through the struggles of childhood. They are both now happily married.

Never underestimate the power of spiritual warfare. When you pray over your children, you are creating a safe spiritual atmosphere for them. In that safe and protected climate, they are protected from evil spirits, and they will be able to grow up into shameless sexuality.

But no parenting advice—no matter how wise—will do you much good if you yourself are not living according to God's plan. To that end, let's take a look at how you can better answer God's call to live a life of shameless sexuality.

Standards for Personal Wisdom

All of us need wisdom for our own personal lives. And there are some simple standards we can adopt to help us walk in shameless sexuality. Some of these things have been discussed in previous chapters, but this information bears repeating in the context of adopting standards for personal wisdom.

1. Be Careful About Entertainment Choices

Many parents are very careful about the kind of entertainment they allow their children to watch, but they do not have that same standard for themselves. This is foolishness, plain and simple. No one becomes immune to temptation simply by becoming an adult. If you put garbage into your mind, garbage is exactly what is going to eventually come out.

Much of today's entertainment has a lot of inappropriate sexual content. If we expose ourselves to that on a regular basis, we will begin to accept those ideas without even realizing it. For this reason, it is important to be careful about our entertainment choices. In order to live in shameless sexuality, we must guard our hearts and our minds.

2. Have Godly Fellowship and Be Accountable to Others

It is very important to be in relationship with other people and to have someone with whom you are accountable. Remember, the devil thrives in darkness and isolation. Light dispels the darkness, so when you share honestly about your struggles and temptations with a godly friend, the enemy is exposed and defeated.

We all need to have a group of Christian friends we can rely on for strength and encouragement. We are in a battle, and we need each other in order to overcome and win.

It is very sad when someone is surrounded by Christian friends but cannot go to them with his or her struggles and concerns. Men need to go to men for prayer and encouragement. Women need to go to other women with their struggles. We can avoid a lot of needless heartache if we are able to support one another in this way.

A good friend of mine was struggling with a temptation one time, so he came to me for prayer and support. He was becoming more and more attracted to a woman at work, but he did not want to give the devil any ground. So he asked if he could talk to me about it when necessary, and he asked me to pray with him and hold him accountable in that situation.

I agreed, and he was able to navigate the episode without any problem. That is what friends are for.

Men need other men as accountability partners, especially if they are struggling with an issue like pornography. Of course, it is always good for a man to pray with his wife. But if he is struggling with a sexual temptation like pornography, he needs another man to help him with that. Why? Because women just do not understand what a man goes through in that struggle. For the same reason, it is a good idea for a woman who is struggling with a sexual issue to go to another woman for encouragement and support. James 5:16 tells us, "Confess your trespasses to one another, and pray for one another, that you may be healed."

As the world around us becomes darker and more corrupt, we need Christian fellowship more than ever. As we love and support one another, we can find healing from temptation and sin, and live a life of shameless sexuality.

3. Keep Sexual Temptations and Problems Transparent Before the Lord

The devil is always condemning us and making us feel that God will judge us for our sexual temptations and struggles. The enemy tries to keep us separated from God so that he can be in control of our life.

In order to live in shameless sexuality, we absolutely must not allow that to happen. We must always run to God with our sexual struggles, never away from Him.

God's throne is a throne of grace and mercy. No matter what you are dealing with, God understands. He says for you to come boldly to Him so that He can give you mercy and grace every time you need it (see Heb. 4:16). When you keep your sexual temptations transparent before God, He is always there, giving you the power to overcome.

I have learned this from personal experience in my own life, since the devil tempts me just as he tempts everyone else. Ungodly thoughts come to my mind, and I find myself in a battle with temptation. I have learned that if I run to God immediately with those thoughts, they vanish.

The Bible says He loves those who speak the truth that is in their hearts. He loves those who live openly and honestly before Him. So when I am tempted, I go to God immediately and I am totally honest with Him. I tell God the thought that has just come to my mind, no matter how ugly or appalling that thought might be. I bring it before God's throne of grace and ask for His help in my time of need. And when I do that, He always gives me the grace I need to take that thought captive.

When you are tempted, the wisest thing you can do is run to God. He has all wisdom, and He is all love and mercy. He will give you the grace you need every time you need it. He will give you the grace to overcome temptation and live a life of shameless sexuality.

4. Do Not Behave or Speak Inappropriately

One day, I walked into a restaurant and saw a friend sitting with an attractive woman who was not his wife. He introduced her to me as a business associate of his, and he explained that they were having a "business" lunch. My first thought was that Karen would kill me if she ever found me having lunch alone with this woman. My second thought was that this was not a healthy situation.

This man ended up being unfaithful to his wife—with more than one woman. That is not surprising. He was very unwise to allow himself to be alone with a beautiful woman, and even more unwise if he thought that would not lead to further temptation and sin.

To stay out of the devil's territory, we need only follow simple wisdom, and much of it is just common sense.

First, never go out to lunch alone with a person of the opposite sex. If it is a "business" lunch, insist that other "business" people join you. This healthy boundary will prevent an unhealthy situation from developing.

Second, if we are going to stay out of temptation and sin, we must have boundaries. There is an appropriate way to relate to members of the opposite sex, and there is also an inappropriate way. In my own personal life, I have set boundaries regarding how I approach, talk to and touch others—particularly women. I will not cross those boundaries, because I do not want to give the devil any place in my life.

When people cross those lines, they risk becoming too familiar with the opposite sex, and they risk inviting temptation and sin.

In church, at work, in the family and in our neighborhoods, it is a good idea for us to set boundaries when it comes to how we relate to members of the opposite sex. For if we allow the wisdom of God to rule our conduct, we can steer clear of temptation and live in shameless sexuality.

victory step #3:
keeping the marriage bond sacred

One of the most important standards of living in shameless sexuality is to keep the marriage bond sacred. If we step outside of His plan for sex, we are stepping into shame and heartache. This is why we must not allow anything to defile the marriage bed. The Bible clearly tells us how important this is to God: "Marriage is honorable among all, and the bed undefiled; but fornicators and adulterers God will judge" (Heb. 13:4).

We live in a world in which marriage is lightly esteemed, if it is esteemed at all. But according to the Bible, marriage is honorable, and sex is the sign of the covenant of marriage. It is sacred. Anyone who defiles marriage can expect to experience judgment.

Sadly, it is estimated that half of all marriages in our society will be affected by adultery. Even more marriages than that will experience mental or emotional adultery. Jesus tells us that if we look at someone with lust, we have already committed adultery in our heart (see Matt. 5:27–28). Long before the physical act of adultery takes place, mental and emotional adultery has already occurred. This type of adultery is even more commonplace in our day when pornography and all sorts of illicit entertainment bombard us from every side.

When a man looks at pornography and fantasizes about a woman other than his wife, he is committing adultery. When a woman fantasizes about a relationship with a man other than her husband, she is committing adultery.

Any time another person, real or imagined, is invited into your sex life, the sacred bond of marriage has been defiled. And this activity does nothing to improve sexual fulfillment. It just brings the baggage of sin into something God wants to be beautiful and pure.

Keeping wedlock sacred means acknowledging that sex is special and that it is something to be shared only between two people who are married to each other.

Keeping your marriage bed undefiled means you will not allow yourself to think about anyone but your spouse before, during or after sex. Keeping your marriage bed undefiled means no pornography or racy material is used to arouse or entertain. Keeping your marriage bed undefiled means the love and devotion of the two marriage partners is all that is needed for sexual intimacy to be the amazing experience God created it to be.

Orgasm or Soulgasm?

The world today can't seem to get enough information about orgasm. Even while waiting to pay for groceries, I am bombarded with headlines claiming to have some new "trick" about how to have the best orgasm ever. This is very sad, because that approach to sex is never fulfilling.

A sex addict has more orgasms than anyone else, but she is never satisfied. A person addicted to pornography or masturbation has more and more orgasms all the time—but the more he has, the less satisfied he becomes. Their selfish search for sexual fulfillment becomes an endless journey of disappointment.

Sex as God designed it is not the product of knowing the latest technique. Rather, sex as God designed it is the beautiful result of two people loving one another and serving one another unselfishly. When their two souls unite in an act of selfless love, sex is very fulfilling.

I often recommend the book *Intimate Issues* by Linda Dillow and Lorraine Pintus, because it explains how an orgasm is never truly satisfying until it is the result of two people focusing on each other and loving each other. The authors of this book call this "soulgasm." When two people are thinking about no one but each other, and only desire to please and love one another, they will not just have an orgasm—they will also have a soulgasm. A soulgasm is the only orgasm that can truly satisfy sexual need.

This reflects the reality that the ultimate sexual experience is sex the way that God created it to be, within the covenant bond of marriage. It is essential to keep that bond undefiled, reserved for your spouse and no one else. In sacred wedlock, sex is not selfish and demanding. It is a precious gift you want to shower upon your spouse, with a love and tenderness that is reserved for him or her alone. It is beautiful and fulfilling—it is the shameless sexuality God designed.

victory step #4:
being a salt-and-light witness

It is true that God has given us the gift of sex to enjoy. But it is important to remember that sex is about more than just "us."

We have a responsibility to represent God with the gift of sexuality and to be a witness to His purposes in this earth. I call this "being a salt-and-light witness." Jesus tells us that we are "salt" and we are "light":

> You are the salt of the earth; but if the salt loses its flavor, how shall it be seasoned? It is then good for nothing but to be thrown out and trampled underfoot by men. You are the light of the world. A city that is set on a hill cannot be hidden. Nor do they light a lamp and put it under a basket, but on a lampstand, and it gives light to all who are in the house. Let your light so shine before men, that they may see your good works and glorify your Father in heaven (Matt. 5:13–16).

When refrigeration was not available, salt was used to preserve food. So when Jesus calls us "salt," He is calling us a *preservative*. He is making it clear that our influence prevents this earth from becoming corrupted by sin.

Jesus also calls us "light." The devil cannot keep the whole world in darkness, because we are here and we are light. Jesus commands us to let our light shine so that people recognize that we are different—that we are children of the Lord, seeking to live out His amazing plan for human sexuality.

The way we handle our sexuality is a very important way to be "salt" and "light." The way we talk, dress and act will either "preserve" God's design for sex or put our stamp of approval on the devil's work of sin and sexual corruption in this earth.

Which will it be?

Take a Stand

If we do not take a stand to represent God, Jesus said we are like salt that has lost its flavor. He said that kind of salt isn't good for anything—you might as well throw it away.

The truth is, this world is suffering terribly from the onslaught of the enemy. The devil is holding many people in sexual bondage, simply because they do not realize there is any other way.

If we do not take a stand for the truth of God, no one will.

If we do not show the world there is a better way through the grace of God, they have no way of finding out.

If we talk just as dirty as the people around us, we are robbing those people of the opportunity to see a better way.

If we are no different from the world around us, we are salt that has lost its flavor—its purpose.

You may work in an environment that is characterized by a lot of crude speech, profanity or immoral behavior. You might be the only person there representing God's way of doing things. You might be the only person who can show others that God has a different plan for sexuality.

In some work environments it seems most people are involved in immorality: adultery, fornication, pornography—you name it! One man told me that if his corporation fired everyone who views pornography during work hours, there wouldn't be enough workers left to run the company.

Sin can take over any workplace atmosphere if it is allowed to do so. In fact, a business can become permeated with the spirit of adultery and divorce. People start to talk loosely about sex, then go out for drinks after work and, before you know it, adultery and lust thrive. Sin becomes almost contagious.

If you are working in that kind of environment every day, you are under a great deal of pressure to act as though you agree with that lifestyle of sin. You must make a decision today—resolve that you are going to be salt and light. When someone starts to tell a dirty joke, you can excuse yourself from the conversation. When someone starts to talk about sexual experiences, you can politely tell that person you are not interested in hearing about it.

There's no need to make people feel condemned or to have a holier-than-thou attitude, but you can kindly let people know that there is another way to live. The apostle Paul talked about this in his letter to the Ephesians. He let us know that the way we talk about sex is a very important part of our witness:

> But fornication and all uncleanness or covetousness, let it not even be named among you, as is fitting for saints; neither filthiness, nor foolish talking, not coarse jesting, which are not fitting, but rather giving of thanks (Eph. 5:3–4).

When I worked in a secular environment, often I found myself in the company of men who told dirty jokes. I would simply walk away. While the subject of sex does not make me uncomfortable in the least, if I am in a group of men who are making sexual jokes or bragging about their latest sexual exploits, I do not join in with that conversation.

Why? It is not that I think I am better than everyone else—I've been there, done that. But when Jesus Christ came into my life, He set me free from sexual sin! He made me a new creature and showed me a better way to live. Now I want to represent Him in every area of my life. I want to show His goodness to others in everything I do and say.

If someone wants to hear about God's plan for sex, I will be happy to talk about it. I will gladly tell them that married sex is the best sex in the world! But I will not participate in a conversation that reinforces the devil's portrayal of sex.

Because I am a public figure, there is a chance I will be recognized when I go places. I keep this in mind whenever I make a decision because I want to be salt and light in this earth. For example, it might be all right for me to see a certain movie, but I consider the effect it could have on others if they saw me watching it. If that movie could be a stumbling block for someone else, I won't go. It's not about "me" and what I want. It's about representing Christ to others. It's about helping others live for Him.

You also represent Christ. You also are called to bring others into relationship with Him. You cannot do this unless you are willing to stand against sexual sin.

You do not need to be legalistic or judgmental. You do need to be mindful of others in the choices you make. People are watching your life. You may be the only Christian—the only salt or light—they will ever encounter.

It is important to stand up for God's ways whenever possible. We have opportunities every day to make our lives a reflection of the goodness and holiness of God.

For instance, one of the pastors at our church was at the mall with his children, and they passed a lingerie store with a very inappropriate, pornographic window display. He was not shopping at that store, but he went in anyway and asked to speak to the manager.

He said, "I am not shopping here today, but I am walking through the mall with my family. Those pictures you have in the window are very inappropriate, and I do not want my children to see that when they come to the mall." The manager was very gracious about it and took the pictures down.

By being salt and light in that situation, this man was able to have a positive influence, not just upon his family, but also upon others.

You may say, "That is such a little thing. What difference does it make?"

It makes all the difference! The only thing keeping the world from total corruption is us! We are the preservative—we are the salt and the light. We do not have to be mean or self-righteous in dealing with people. But holding up a higher standard for the world to see is our responsibility. We must let others know that God has a better plan—a more amazing plan—for our sexuality.

Being a Light in the Public Arena

The devil is trying his best to legitimize gay marriage in our country. But in the 2004 election, gay marriage was voted down in 11 states—and media pundits gave the credit to "values voters." These voters were Christians who decided to stand up and be "salt" in the making of public policy.

They could have just "gone with the flow" of our society. Had they done that, the devil would have been allowed to keep advancing his strategy to drag our society into further darkness and corruption. Instead, Christians held back those forces of darkness. By standing up for God's ways, by being salt and light, these Christians preserved an atmosphere of godliness for everyone.

The devil tirelessly works to use human sexuality to achieve his own twisted purposes. So we must be working also. We must make the decision to be "salt" and "light" in this earth. We must help the world understand that sex as God created it to be is shameless and beautiful.

CHAPTER 21

victory step #5:
engaging in spiritual warfare

Like it or not, we are in a war. We have an invisible enemy who never stops trying to steal, kill and destroy us. He is relentless in his efforts. The Bible tells us just what we must do to combat his tactics: "Be sober, be vigilant; because your adversary the devil walks about like a roaring lion seeking whom he may devour" (1 Pet. 5:8).

We must be sober and vigilant. We must know our enemy. He is the same enemy that stalked Adam and Eve in the Garden.

Remember, he never shows up as the ugly demon he really is. He shows up as a harmless person or situation. Perhaps the devil comes in the form of an alluring woman, an attractive man or the promise that illicit sex will satisfy you.

But we are not helpless pawns in the game of life. No. We do not have to sit by and allow the devil to mow down our lives! Jesus gave us authority to *trample* over *all* the power of the devil: "I give you the authority to trample on serpents and scorpions, and over all the power of the enemy, and nothing shall by any means hurt you" (Luke 10:19). He said that *nothing* the devil does will be able to harm us. He can't ruin our lives unless we let him, because we have the authority, from Jesus Himself, to win the battle against him.

That is very good news. We have the advantage—we have Jesus on our side. Believers ought to be rejoicing—and winning!

It seems, however, that many Christians don't yet understand that truth—the devil is trampling them into the ground. They are not *using* the authority Jesus has given them.

In order to crush the devil, we must *take* that authority and *use it!*

Pick Up Your Sword

The Bible tells us that the weapons of our warfare are mighty through God. We can pick them up at any time and use them effectively. But we do have to actually use them! Remember, a soldier can have the best weapon in the world, but if he doesn't shoulder that rifle and fire it at the advancing enemy, it won't do him a bit of good.

In the same way, we must use the weapons God has given us. We must take up the full armor of God and do warfare for our children, our spouse and ourselves.

> Stand therefore, having girded your waist with truth, having put on the breastplate of righteousness, and having shod your feet with the preparation of the gospel of peace; above all, taking the shield of faith with which you will be able to quench all the fiery darts of the wicked one. And take the helmet of salvation, and the sword of the Spirit, which is the word of God; praying always with all prayer and supplication in the Spirit, being watchful to this end (Eph. 6:14–18).

Truth, righteousness, peace, faith, salvation, the Word of God and *prayer* are not just abstract concepts. These are spiritual weapons that will quench the devil's fiery darts—every time. I believe two of our most powerful weapons are "the sword of the Spirit, which is the Word of God" and "praying always." These weapons pack a nuclear punch!

When we fire those "nuclear" weapons of God's Word, praying at all times "in the Spirit," we can put the enemy to flight in a hurry.

Employ the Power of Binding and Loosing

The Bible tells us to pray all the time and to be watchful. In the day in which we live, that is more necessary than ever. We must pray diligently every day for our children, marriage, spouse and all our loved ones.

If your spouse is struggling with sexual sin, you must do spiritual warfare for him or her. If you are struggling with sexual sin yourself, go to war with the devil for your own freedom. You have the authority to bind the devil, so use it! Jesus said, "Whatever you bind on earth will be bound in heaven, and whatever you loose on earth will be loosed in heaven" (Matt. 18:18).

You don't have to let the devil mess with you or your family!

You can bind him through prayer. That's right! When you know your authority in God, you can say with all confidence, "I bind a spirit of adultery from my spouse. I bind every spirit of pornography from my family. I bind every spirit of lust from my children."

Jesus promised that whatever you bind on Earth is bound in heaven. In other words, by calling upon the name and power of Jesus, binding those spirits is a "done deal"—they will no longer be able to harass your family.

The Power of Agreement

Jesus said that even more power is available when a husband and a wife get together in prayer and agree with each other: "Again I say to you that if two of you agree on earth concerning anything that they ask, it will be done for them by My Father in heaven" (Matt. 18:19). A husband and wife can lock the devil out of their home if they agree together in prayer. The Father will give them anything they ask, when they agree about it.

What a powerful weapon!

All of us who are married should take advantage of this amazing weapon and use the prayer of agreement to protect our home and children from the devil's attacks. Now more than ever we must utilize every weapon at our disposal to protect our families and walk in sexual purity.

CHAPTER 22

victory step #6:
meditating on the bible

To understand sexual freedom or any other kind of freedom, we must realize that the battlefield of victory is the mind. Further, it's very important we recognize that when Jesus died on the cross, He won the victory for us.

When they crucified Jesus, they nailed Him to a cross and placed it on a hill called Golgotha. The word "Golgotha" means "the place of a skull." I've been to Jerusalem and seen Golgotha. It is eerie. As you view this hill from a distance, it looks just like a human skull. Therefore, on the day Jesus was crucified, He was hanging on a cross, positioned prominently on the top of a hill shaped like a skull. This was no accident. It was divinely orchestrated by God to reveal to the world the reason Christ died: to save us through the transformation and freeing of our hearts and *minds.*

This powerful picture cannot be overlooked. Jesus died to save us and set us free. Our minds are the battleground in the fight for our salvation and resulting freedom. The truth of the matter is, until our minds are set free, we're not free. Until the transforming power of the blood of Jesus and the water of His Word flow upon our minds, we are in bondage.

Enter the Battlefield

Francis Frangipane once said, "A bondage is a house of thoughts." This is a truth we must understand if we are going to win the battle for freedom.

When it comes to sexual bondage, many people think the issue is primarily biological or hormonal. Therefore, they try to fight their sexual impulses through physical discipline or willpower. Even the strongest person with the greatest amount of willpower can only last for a certain period of time when confronted with the force of sexual temptation. Thousands of years of human history prove that sexual sin can take the best people down.

When it comes to sexual sin, you have to deal with the root issue before you can find a real solution. In other words, if you have a problem but are unaware of the true source of it, either you will try false answers that don't work or you will believe that no answer exists. In the area of sexual temptation and bondage, you will never be set free until you deal with the root issue: the way you think.

Here is what Jesus says concerning freedom: "Then Jesus said to those Jews who believed Him, 'If you abide in My word, you are My disciples indeed. And you shall know the truth, and the truth shall make you free'" (John 8:31–32). Jesus clearly states that true freedom is the result of abiding in His Word. He promises that if we become committed disciples of His Word, we will "know" the truth, and the result will be freedom. But the word "know" here doesn't just mean "to understand"—it means "to experience intimately." Therefore, Jesus promised that if we will commit our minds and hearts to His Word, the result will be a personal experience that sets us free.

We also need to realize that the battle isn't between us and the devil. Even though our minds are the battlefield, the real fight is between God's Word and Satan. As long as we think the issue is about us, we will try to fight it ourselves. We must understand that we are helpless against Satan without God's Word. As already stated, Ephesians 6:17 tells us that the Word is our "sword of the Spirit" in our fight against the forces of darkness. Even if we hate the enemy and are willing to fight, without God's Word, we are doomed to defeat and bondage.

Not everyone has the same bondages. However, you show me a person who doesn't live with a close, personal dependence on God's Word, and I'll show you someone who is defeated and in bondage. The bondage might not be sex, but fear, depression, hate or something else. No one is the exception—not even Jesus.

Chapter 4 of Matthew records the temptation of Christ after His 40 days of fasting in the wilderness. In Jesus' weakest moment, Satan appeared to attack Him. What weapon did he use? Thoughts! Three times Satan attacked Jesus with half-truths and seductive offers. Every time, Jesus countered with a response beginning with, "It is written." Demonstrating the awesome power of God's Word over Satan's best attack, Jesus won and taught us how to do the same.

The apostle Paul gives us rare spiritual insight to help us understand the battle of our minds and how it is won.

> For though we walk in the flesh, we do not war according to the flesh. For the weapons of our warfare are not carnal but mighty in God for pulling down strongholds, casting down arguments and every high thing that exalts itself against the knowledge of God, *bringing every thought into captivity to the obedience of Christ* (2 Cor. 10:3–5, emphasis added).

These verses accurately describe the reality of the battlefield of our minds and the way to win the war for our freedom. Yet let's face it—it's hard for us to believe in the power of weapons that are invisible. It's also difficult for us to fight an enemy we can't see. However, that is exactly what we must do if we are going to live in victory. Paul tells us that we have weapons of warfare available for us that are "not carnal." Our weapons are not physical or natural; they are spiritual and invisible. He goes on to say that these weapons are "mighty in God for pulling down strongholds."

God has given us powerful spiritual weapons to overcome every stronghold Satan has brought into our lives to keep us in bondage. However, the power of these weapons will work only in an atmosphere of faith in which we are willing to obediently wage a battle for our minds.

Look again at Paul's language in 2 Corinthians 10. He tells us that we must bring every thought captive to the obedience of Christ. This literally means that every thought in our minds must submit to the authority of Jesus Christ—the Word (see John 1:1). Any thought we won't take captive will take us captive by building strongholds of "arguments" and "high things that exalt themselves against the knowledge of God." By faith, we must fight against any and every thought that won't bow its knee to Christ—such thoughts are our real enemy.

How do we defeat that enemy, particularly when it comes to sexual sin? Through biblical meditation. The Word of God is the only force powerful enough to destroy the strongholds of unrighteous thoughts that Satan introduces into our minds to hold us in bondage. It also acts as "sacred software" to reprogram us to function in the truth as God intended. The human brain is an amazing computer. However, we are all born with software problems, viruses and glitches that only the Word can fix. The continuing process of biblical meditation as a discipline in our lives is crucial for freedom to be secured and maintained.

The battle for freedom is waged in "the place of a skull." So until your mind is completely surrendered to Christ, and you are willing to seek and accept His Word as truth, you aren't ready for freedom and can't obtain it by any other means. However, if you're willing to bring your mind to Christ and cast down the arguments (thoughts that reject the truth of God's Word), surrender the high things (prideful thinking that believes it has a better answer than God's Word,) and bring every thought captive, you are ready for freedom.

The Promise of Biblical Meditation

The book of Psalms begins with this powerful description of the person who has committed his or her mind to biblical meditation:

> Blessed is the man
> Who walks not in the counsel of the ungodly,
> Nor stands in the path of sinners,
> Nor sits in the seat of the scornful;
> But his delight is in the law of the LORD,
> And in His law he meditates day and night.
> He shall be like a tree
> Planted by the rivers of water,
> That brings forth its fruit in its season,
> Whose leaf also shall not wither;
> And whatever he does shall prosper (1:1–3).

The power of biblical meditation is so great that God promises that everything we do will prosper if we will practice it "day and night." Can you imagine everything in your life prospering and succeeding?

Psalm 1:3 compares a person who meditates on Scripture day and night to a tree planted by a river. The tree doesn't have to worry whether or not the rains come because it has a constant source of water to keep it healthy and fruitful. The result is guaranteed success—which is what God promises all of us if we will meditate on Scripture.

If biblical meditation was the most difficult thing you ever did in your life, wouldn't it be worthwhile if it guaranteed you success in everything you did—work, money, relationships, sex, and so on? When I first heard about it, I thought to myself, *I don't think I can do that.* I also thought, *I don't know if I want to do that!* Sure, I loved God and believed in the Bible, but to think about it all day and night—wow! I didn't think I was up to it.

That was 20 years ago. Now, I can't believe how hard it was *not* doing it. I regret every day that I spent in unbelief and procrastination. It caused me so much needless defeat and suffering.

Misunderstanding the idea of biblical meditation scares most people away. They think it is either impractical or too spiritually difficult for them. The truth is, any man, woman or child can meditate upon Scripture day and night. In this chapter, I'll correct the misunderstandings concerning this powerful practice and also provide practical insight regarding how to integrate it into your demanding lifestyle.

Regardless of what you've experienced in your past, your future can be full of great blessing and success. One great blessing is the power to live in sexual purity.

Let me share with you a powerful truth concerning your mind and sexual temptation. Did you know that you cannot take a thought out of your mind? That's right—it's impossible. This is why sexual temptation is so wearying to try to fight.

Let me illustrate: You're flipping through TV channels, and all of a sudden there she is a—a perfect 10—she's gorgeous, sexy and looking at *you* with that sultry stare. For a minute, you take it all in. Later, you turn off the television, but she is still in your mind. You lie in bed thinking about her.

Realizing what you're doing is wrong, you being feeling guilty. However, the more you try to get that thought out of your mind, the worse it gets. Other sexual images begin to surface in your mind, and the battle is raging. Finally, you give in to a mental gallery of erotic images that arouse you. Defeated and guilty, you go to sleep, only to wake up to another day of the same futile battle. *I want to live for God,* you think, *but will I ever be able to overcome these kinds of thoughts?*

The answer is yes. You can have the power to overcome undesirable thoughts and exercise complete control over your mind. To do so, you must remember this: You cannot take thoughts out of your mind, but you can crowd them out with more powerful thoughts. This is where biblical meditation comes in.

Most people wrestle constantly with their thought lives. Many times we know the things we think about are wrong, but we don't know how to stop them. And this is true not only of sexual thoughts but also of thoughts related to worry, fear, anger, and so on. The more we try to stop thinking about them, the more they occupy our thinking. Satan loves this vicious cycle because he wants to turn our minds inward until they wear out, we give up, and he controls us. Efforts to change seem futile, so we just give in and become like everyone else. Many people turn to alcohol, drugs and/or pleasure. It is the only way they know to cope with their internal misery.

Before I came into the ministry, I worked in my family's business. On my way to work every day, I passed a billboard advertising a swimming pool company. It was a very large sign with a woman in a swimsuit filling most of it. Whoever painted her was intimately familiar with the female body and went to great pains to include every detail. As I passed the sign each day, I looked. In fact, I would slow down before I got to it, hoping to hit a red light so that I could look longer. Finally, the image on that billboard became a permanent fixture in my thinking.

One morning as I was trying to pray, that image flashed in my mind. Immediately, I confessed it to the Lord and told Him that I didn't want to think about it anymore but that I didn't know how to stop it.

The Lord spoke to my heart right then and said something that set me on the road to freedom from sexual temptation. He said to me, "Whenever this thought or any other temptation comes into your mind, begin to meditate on My Word." From that moment on, I began overcoming sexual temptation. I'm not saying I never sinned again; I'm saying that I started a pattern of winning more battles than I lost by knowing how to replace bad thoughts with God's thoughts.

You can't get bad thoughts out of your mind with your own thoughts or some method of mind control or distraction. If you do, your success will be short-lived, and the thoughts will come back with a greater strength than before. The only power that can truly set you free from sexual temptation or any other mental battle is biblical meditation. This is why God promises success for the person who has committed to doing it day and night.

Make up your mind right now that the next time a bad thought comes into your mind—sexual or otherwise—you are going to replace it with a Scripture. Even more important, you will realize that the more you meditate on God's Word *before* you are tempted, the fewer opportunities Satan has to tempt you in the first place. You see, biblical meditation fills your mind with God's Word—it is no longer unoccupied territory. As the old saying goes, "An idle mind is the devil's playground." In reality, an idle mind is the devil's battleground where he stalks and defeats his victims.

Knowing how to meditate on the Word of God "day and night" is another important issue. If you misunderstand this point, you will get discouraged and give up before you start. However, once you realize what God's Word is saying, you will see its brilliance and practicality.

To understand this issue, let's look at something God said through Moses to the children of Israel as they were preparing to enter the Promised Land.

> Hear, O Israel: The Lord our God, the Lord is one! You shall love the Lord your God with all your heart, with all your soul, and with all your strength. And these words which I command you today shall be in your heart. You shall teach them diligently to your children, and shall talk of them when you sit in your house, when you walk by the way, when you lie down, and when you rise up (Deut. 6:4–7).

God's first commandment to Israel was for them to love Him and His Word with their whole hearts. You must totally commit yourself to God before you can live victoriously. The second thing God commanded the men of Israel to do was to diligently teach their children the Word of God. To this day, God still holds men responsible to train their children in the Word and ways of God (see Eph. 6:4).

The interesting thing about God's commandment to train children in the Word is that God detailed for them the four times of the day and night when it was to be done. In Deuteronomy 6:7, God directed the men of Israel to teach their children His Word and to talk about it when they (1) were sitting in their houses, (2) were on their way somewhere, (3) rose up in the morning and (4) went to bed at night.

Let's go beyond God's commandment of teaching children. Think about the times when you are tempted and struggle with your thoughts the most. I'll tell you when it is. It is when your mind is in a reflective mode. You probably don't have as many difficulties with your thoughts when you are busy at work. Which isn't to say you can't have problems then; it's just not as common at work because you are mentally preoccupied.

The times when our minds are most open to satanic assault are when we are sitting around our houses (channel surfing, Web surfing and so on), on our way somewhere (in the car looking at billboards, daydreaming), and lying in bed as we wake up and go to sleep (worrying about our problems, fantasizing about our sinful desires). God knew thousands of years ago, before there were televisions, computers, cars, billboards or anything else, that we were most vulnerable at four particular times of the day. He also knew that those same four times were the best opportunities for us to meditate on Scripture in order to learn it ourselves and teach it to our children.

Meditating on God's Word "day and night" means we are committed to occupying our minds with the Word of God during the four reflective times of our day (as mentioned in Deuteronomy 6:7). This doesn't mean we are legalistic and can't watch television, rent a movie, surf the Web or listen to music at these particular times. It just means that God's Word comes before any of those things so that when we encounter a sinful thought we're equipped to take it captive and drown it out with the Word of God.

Life is more pleasant and peaceful when you learn to meditate on Scripture. You realize that you can defeat the enemy any time he comes against you and can live your life free from mental turmoil and sexual sin. As you meditate on it, the Word unfolds within you, and you begin to see its beauty and understand its mysteries. The Word becomes your life source, and you begin longing for it.

A promise of complete success awaits the person who commits to meditating on God's Word day and night. This promise is open for any man, woman or child to claim. Like a tree planted by a river, any person who desires to plant his or her mind in God's Word will never have to worry because the future is settled. Victory and success are guaranteed!

The Process of Biblical Meditation

Biblical meditation is a delightful discipline that adds a new dimension to life. It is not a religious ball and chain; instead, it is a practice that makes life much easier and more enjoyable. It isn't a burden—it's a blessing. Let's discuss how we can practice biblical meditation in a manner that can fit well with our needs and our lifestyle.

Let's begin by understanding the word "meditate" as it is used in the Bible. Obviously, we're not talking about meditation as it's practiced in Eastern religions or the New Age movement, which involves focusing the mind on self, some unknown cosmic power or your choice of gods. Biblical meditation is mentally rehearsing a portion of Scripture that in turn causes you to consider God and the things of God.

The word "meditate" as used in the Bible means two basic things. First, it means "to consider or ponder." Second, it means "to speak or murmur to oneself." A good picture of meditation is an animal such as a cow or sheep that chews its cud and ruminates. Rumination is the process of chewing, swallowing and then regurgitating to chew again.

In the context of biblical meditation, "rumination" means to take a Bible verse, text, chapter or story and put it into your mind. Then, throughout the day, you continue to mentally "chew on it." As you meditate, the Word of God unfolds within you. You begin to see things in the Bible you've never seen before as God's Word gives you a new level of wisdom, insight and encouragement.

Suppose you are facing something at work that you're anxious about. It is causing you to lose sleep at night, have headaches and be in turmoil. Just as a physician prescribes specific medicine for a specific illness, you need to find a Scripture to meditate on that will minister to that need. In the case of worry and anxiety, Matthew 6:25–34 would a great text to meditate on to calm you heart and give you faith to trust God. If meditation becomes some dry, religious exercise, you aren't going to do it. However, if it helps you find solutions, control your thoughts and emotions, and build a deeper relationship with God, it becomes much more desirable. That is the key to making it a permanent discipline in your life.

Another thing I love about biblical meditation is that you can do it anywhere, at any time, and it produces immediate results. On an airplane, in a meeting, at the car wash, you can simply reflect upon the Word and enjoy the presence and power of God instantly. With today's fast-paced, demanding schedules, this is important.

The Bible is so wonderful. It addresses every issue of life and gives us Scriptures for knowledge, wisdom, encouragement, warning and comfort. It equips us to face everyday issues head-on and victoriously.

So, let's talk about some practical steps you can take to make it work in your life.

First of all, you need to have a Bible you can read and understand. There are many good translations of the Bible that are written in today's English. Find one that you like.

A Bible concordance is also helpful during biblical meditation, because it allows you to find the Scripture passages you are looking for. For example, if you're dealing with fear, you can look up the word "fear" in the concordance, and it will show you where that word can be found in the Bible. It also provides the definitions to the original Greek and Hebrew words.

Christian bookstores today have many good Bibles and study tools. Shop around and find something you like. It's well worth the time and money you will spend.

Once you have an understandable translation of the Bible (and concordance, if desired), the next step is to wake up a little earlier and begin your day with a "quiet time" with the Lord. If you can't do it at home, you can have a quiet time in your car or at the office. The main thing is to find a private place where you can spend some time reading your Bible and praying. The morning is a strategically important time for you to prepare to face your day with God and His Word as your allies.

A quiet time can last 10 minutes or 2 hours. The quantity of time, though, is not important. What's important is that you spend time reading the Bible and talking to the Lord about what's happening in your life.

Concerning biblical meditation, your quiet time is when you read a verse, story or text of Scripture for the purpose of "loading" it into your mind for mediation through the day. Again, read what you need. Find something that applies to your life. If you don't have a pressing need, then find a Scripture you want to memorize or a verse you don't understand that you want the Holy Spirit to reveal to you.

Also, if you're being tempted or oppressed, find a Scripture that deals specifically with that issue. Read it through several times. Then pray for the Holy Spirit to give you power to meditate on it and to bring it back to your mind at the right times. Then ask the Holy Spirit to reveal the Scripture to your heart and make it alive to you.

Throughout the day, as you face temptations or when you are in a reflective time—sitting at a stoplight, lying in bed or taking a coffee break at work—you simply bring the Scripture passage(s) back to mind and ponder it. As you do, the Word of God protects your mind against the devil's attacks. If you have a lustful thought, immediately replace it with the Scripture passage. You will immediately experience the Lord's peace.

The presence of God powerfully inhabits His Word. Paul exhorts us to continually invite the Holy Spirit's presence into our lives by speaking or "murmuring" to one another with psalms, hymns and spiritual songs from our hearts to God (see Eph. 5:18-19). As we do this, the Holy Spirit inhabits our words and praises. The result is a continual flow of the power and peace of God in our life. Truly, speaking and singing to ourselves as we focus on God and His Word takes meditation to a higher level. Incorporating this as a habit as we go through our day is a pleasant and practical way to enforce the discipline of biblical meditation.

If you meditate on God's Word day and night, He has promised you success in everything you do. Begin your day by putting Scripture into your mind, and regularly reflect on it. You'll then be equipped to face any challenge of life successfully. Over time, your mind will be transformed. The result is thinking and behavior that is faith-filled, Bible-based and victorious.

Begin today right where you are. What issues are you facing? Where is Satan attacking you? There is a Scripture that can empower you to overcome and succeed. It is waiting for you in the Bible. As you read it and then meditate on it, you will enter into a new dimension of Christian living. You will find that you are empowered to overcome Satan's deceptions, particularly those related to sexual temptation. The Fig Leaf Conspiracy will no longer have any effect on your life.

As biblical meditation becomes part of your daily routine, your life will become richer and more peaceful than you ever imagined.

And as you employ these six standards in your life, Satan's conspiracy will have no room to operate. You can begin to experience tremendous joy and greater freedom in your marriage relationship.

PART V

the keys to
sexual fulfillment
in marriage

experiencing sexual pleasure in your marriage

Now that we've discovered how to live a life of shameless sexuality, let's talk about how to experience sexual pleasure in your marriage relationship.

We have seen how God designed marriage to be an intimate union between a man and a woman that would be filled and fueled by sexual pleasure and delight. Sex is God's creation and His desire is for us to enjoy it to its fullest within the marriage relationship.

We must also remember that all of the scriptural prohibitions against sexual sin and perversions are not given by God to keep us from having fun or being fulfilled. Every biblical warning is there to keep us from heartache and destruction. God's motive is love, not legalism. And as we have seen, though many people in our society boast of "sexual freedoms" that violate the warnings of Scripture, their lives invariably prove the fact that the wage of sin is still death!

The awful affects of the Fig Leaf Conspiracy are clearly seen in today's sexually permissive society: a myriad of sexually transmitted diseases, adultery, dysfunctional relationships, broken hearts and shattered dreams.

While those fully immersed in this confused and fallen world accuse God of being anti-sex, we know God Himself created sex and that He is the one who designed it to be so exciting and pleasurable. Those who don't understand this truth are easily deceived into believing they must visit the realm of sin to really experience sexual pleasure and fulfillment.

Yet in counseling over the years, I have seen countless couples devastated or divorced because one or both of them crossed the line sexually—usually in a vain search for pleasure, intimacy or validation. Sin always destroys whatever it touches.

The truth is, sex in marriage is wonderful. God wants us to enjoy it to its fullest. Nevertheless, countless Christians wonder if a truly spiritual person has any business thinking about sex or enjoying it without reservation. Again, the devil encourages this kind of thinking, as it is an integral part of his conspiracy code. The enemy wants us to believe that if we are good Christians, we just won't be very sexual. But just the opposite is true.

God created us with a threefold nature: body, soul and spirit. Being spiritual doesn't mean we deny our nature as sexual beings created by God. It means that we submit every area of our lives to the lordship of Christ in order to fulfill His desire for us. And God's desire for our bodies is that we be blessed through the enjoyment of sex in an intimate marriage relationship.

Now that we've discussed the "what" regarding our sexuality, let's take some time to explore the "how."

If you're like most Christian couples, you aren't exactly sure how to experience sexual fulfillment. To that end, I'd like to share three important keys that will open the door to God's best for you and your spouse!

CHAPTER 24

key #1:
understanding sexual differences between men and women

When Karen and I first got married, I was completely ignorant concerning the inherent sexual differences between us. In addition to my ignorance, I had also been deceived by pornography, locker-room lies and media portrayals of sex. I was a sexual problem waiting for a place to happen. Therefore, even though Karen and I were attracted to each other and had an active marital sex life, we both experienced frustration because of false sexual expectations. It took years before we finally understood our differences and began to respect them.

As we grew in understanding and respect for our differences, our sexual intimacy and pleasure grew dramatically. No longer were we placing unrealistic expectations on each other—or expecting one another to act in ways that were contrary to our nature.

It made all the difference for us!

Visual or Emotional Stimulation

The first important realization we made was that men are visually stimulated, and women are emotionally stimulated. Women are by no means blind as it relates to sex, but they have a much greater capacity for responding to emotional stimulation. This is hard for men to understand. Because of this, many men don't take the time to talk to their wives and patiently meet their emotional and romantic needs.

This lack of emotional support costs men dearly in the area of sex.

Every man must realize that his wife isn't going to turn *on* sexually just because he takes his clothes *off*. Women turn on because their husbands talk to them throughout the day and pay attention to them. Women rarely respond to sex beyond the state of their emotions. This doesn't mean that a woman can't give herself to her husband sexually if she doesn't feel like it. It simply means that her emotional nature is an integral part of her sexuality.

In understanding why God made women this way, we must understand that God is concerned about the overall integrity of the relationship, not just about sex. Therefore, God designed sex in marriage to reach its potential only if genuine care and sensitivity are part of the relationship. In His divine genius, God created a system that ensures that jerks don't get good sex.

The best sex in the world is achieved by respecting the differences in our spouse. Concerning women, this means that a man cares for his wife in a sensitive and sacrificial manner. This includes the all-important ingredient of romance, which simply means that a husband initiates behavior that pleases his wife and meets her needs and desires. When a husband does this, his wife becomes sexually open and responsive to him.

Concerning a man's sexual nature, men are very visual. Even though women may have a problem understanding this, it is an undeniable fact. To fulfill her husband's sexual desires, a woman must realize that he wants to see her naked body. Even though flannel nightgowns and pitch-black bedrooms are the sexual refuge for many women who don't want to expose themselves, they are the archenemy of sexual fulfillment for men. Just as a man needs to understand and meet his wife's emotional needs, a woman must respect and fulfill her husband's visual needs. This means going outside of her comfort zone to wear attractive lingerie before sex and to expose her body to her husband before and during sex for his satisfaction.

To understand the differences between men and women in the area of sex, all you need to do is look at how they sin. Men turn to pornography that wrongfully feeds their visual need, and women turn to soap operas and romance novels that wrongfully feed their emotional need.

Rather than pursuing fulfillment sinfully outside of the relationship with our spouse, we must learn to respect each other's differences and meet each other's needs within the intimacy of marriage.

Sexual Touching Versus Nonsexual Affection

Men need sexual touching, and women need nonsexual affection. This issue is one of the most confusing differences in men and women. When we don't understand this basic difference between us, sex becomes a bittersweet battle of the wills. The common scenario that is played out in countless bedrooms is an aggressive husband roughly groping his wife as she complains and subsequently retreats into a sexually defensive posture. The result is that both their needs are denied, and they end up frustrated.

To be fulfilled in sex, a man must understand that his wife needs soft, nonsexual touching throughout the day and during sex. Such affectionate touching makes her feel valued and emotionally cared for. The more nonsexual affection a man gives his wife, the more sexually responsive she becomes.

This is the opposite of the way a man is designed and thinks. That is why most men think that the way to turn on their wives is the way they are turned on—by direct sexual touching. That is why most men fail to elicit an enthusiastic sexual response from their wives. On the other hand, a woman needs to understand that her husband desires direct sexual touching. It is very satisfying and stimulating for a man and satisfies a deep need in him.

Therefore, when husbands and wives understand each other and respect their differing natures, their times of intimacy will involve both affectionate caressing and direct sexual stimulation.

Obviously, as sexual intensity builds, a woman also wants and needs direct stimulation. This can be achieved in a number of ways, but it must always be done in a tender manner that satisfies her desire and doesn't ignore her overall need for soft, nonsexual affection. Of course, a wife may want her husband to touch and caress specific parts of her body, such as her breasts and vaginal area. Again, such caressing must always be pleasing to her.

The most dangerous element that threatens sexual fulfillment is selfishness. When couples refuse to accept their sexual differences, they ensure that they will both be doomed to frustration and dissatisfaction.

The best sex happens when both the man and the wife try hard to meet each other's needs. Two sexually sensitive and selfless people will reach the most complete sexual fulfillment in marriage.

Differing Levels of Desire

Men and women have different levels of sexual need and achieve orgasms differently. The majority of men are more sexual than their wives. This means they think about sex more and have a more intense need for it more often. This is especially true among younger men, those between 18 and 45 years of age.

As women age, their desire for sex often increases. Some of this is because of a greater emotional security in their marriages. Also, the absence of the fear of pregnancy and/or a greater acceptance of their sexuality can cause women to become more sexually open.

As men age, their testosterone level gradually drops, which causes a decrease in sexual desire. This change usually begins to be noticed when a man is in his forties or fifties. Therefore, throughout the life of a marriage, it is possible for either spouse to desire sex more often or less often than the other. Seldom will their desires be exactly the same. In general, it is the man who desires sex more than his wife, but I have counseled many a frustrated wife whose husband was uninterested in sex.

The main point in saying all of this is to illustrate the need for us to be accepting of each other even though we may not have the same sexual intensity or need simultaneously. It is devastating for either a husband or a wife to be judged, ignored or rejected by a spouse when expressing a sexual need. Our needs are an inherent part of us. Therefore, when we reject our spouses' needs, we reject them.

I'll never forget the young couple I counseled who were on the verge of splitting up. The crux of their problem was that she was put out by his regular need for sex. As I listened to him tell his side of the story, I heard a normal young husband expressing his desire for sex with his wife and the rejection and shame he felt from her. As I listened to his wife tell her side of the story, I heard her saying that she didn't accept his sexuality. She fully expected that he would rarely need sex. As a result, she flatly rejected his advances as she accused him of being perverted for wanting so much sex.

Regardless of how much shame or rejection couples heap upon each other, sex is a deep need, especially in men. When this need is understood and accepted, good will and intimacy are shared between a man and woman. When it is misunderstood and rejected, serious problems and sexual frustration result.

Is Orgasm Necessary for Sexual Fulfillment?

The next step in accepting how we differ in our sexual responsiveness is to understand the role that orgasm plays in sexual fulfillment. Men have an orgasm when they ejaculate—which means they must achieve orgasm to experience sexual fulfillment. However, women can have sex with their husbands without experiencing an orgasm. This is because a woman's primary sexual organ that produces an orgasm is her clitoris, and it is located outside and above her vagina. Yet even though she often doesn't have an orgasm during sex, the wife can still be sexually satisfied. This is difficult for most men to understand, but it is nevertheless true.

Even though she can enjoy sex without an orgasm, most women desire orgasms on a regular basis. When a woman has the desire to achieve an orgasm, she needs to express this to her husband and guide him to stimulate her properly.

For a husband to meet his wife's need to achieve an orgasm, he must slow down, be gentle and listen to her. Some men selfishly rush into sex and only care about getting their own needs met. The result is that their wives feel used and sexually frustrated. Men must understand that women warm up to sex more slowly. They require attention before, during and after sex in order to experience sexual climax and fulfillment.

Men can become sexually aroused almost instantly. Therefore, men often try to rush their wives into having a sexual response, but women just don't work that way in the bedroom. As I heard Gary Smalley say, "In the world of sex, men are microwave ovens and women are crock pots." This is a universal truth. Regardless of how men are sexually wired, they must realize that their wives are different and require the proper attention and care before and during sex if they are to reach a climax.

This doesn't mean that all sex in marriage has to be experienced in the same manner. Some sexual needs in marriage can be satisfied through "quickies." This usually means that a spouse (most often a wife) offers her body to her partner for the sake of meeting an immediate sexual need. A "quickie" simply means that through intercourse or some other means, sex is achieved in a more spontaneous and timely manner.

However, for a woman to reach an orgasm and to experience full sexual satisfaction, a "quickie" won't suffice. Women need to be romanced and cared for before sex. During sex, a woman needs foreplay, affection, loving communication and the stimulation of her clitoris in a manner that pleases her. In this way, a woman is able to reach an orgasm and attain sexual satisfaction.

Clearly, men and women are very different sexually by design. Understanding these differences and respecting our spouse's sexual nature leads to sexual fulfillment.

key #2:
eliminating common enemies of sexual fulfillment

If couples are going to experience sexual satisfaction for a lifetime, they must properly respond to some common problems that can sabotage their hopes for success. Even though all of these problems can be overcome, they must be taken seriously and addressed properly. Sadly, many couples that marry and have great sexual energy and attraction end up fighting or even divorcing, citing their sexual problems as the primary issue.

Because sexual problems are one of the main reasons for tension between married couples, I will address three common enemies of sexual fulfillment and how you can overcome them.

Unresolved Anger Seethes Beneath the Sheets

Anger is inevitable in every marriage. There is no way two people can live together without becoming angry at each other at some point. Even healthy couples experience anger on a regular basis. This may surprise you, but it's true. The issue isn't whether we will experience anger, but rather, how we deal with it.

I have counseled many couples over the years that have experienced sexual problems—and a good number of them were experiencing sexual difficulties as a result of unresolved anger between them. Indeed, there is a direct connection between our emotions and our sexual responses.

When we successfully resolve issues in our marriage, our sexual connection is unhindered—we are free to express our love to one another in a physical way. But when our personal issues remain unresolved and anger builds up, our sexual desires and responses change. We just don't connect anymore.

That is why I believe unresolved anger is the most dangerous element in marriage.

It is vital that husbands and wives be honest about their emotions and be open to such honesty from each other. Such honesty allows them to resolve their anger and frustration quickly. The apostle Paul in Ephesians 4:26 tells us to admit our anger but not to let the sun go down on it. Sexual health isn't just an issue of how our bodies respond to sexual stimuli. It is very much dependent upon our emotional state. Unresolved anger means feelings of hurt, mistrust or violation exist between us. The more these negative emotions accumulate and remain unexpressed, the more our sense of anger and alienation will be reflected in our sexual relationship.

You see, sex acts as both a thermometer and a thermostat in a marriage.

As a thermostat, sex makes marriage better. Good sex actually increases the emotional temperature of the marriage and builds feelings of intimacy and goodwill. However, it also acts as a thermometer, which means it reflects the state of the relationship. Sexual problems can many times be due to unresolved conflict. A lack of healthy sexual relations for any significant length of time is a warning signal that could reflect unresolved anger between a husband and wife.

If you have unresolved anger in your marriage, you need to talk honestly about your feelings. Commit to forgiving your spouse, and make a decision not to allow anger and bitterness to remain. If you can't resolve an issue or issues between you, get counseling from a Christian leader or professional. Your marriage is too important to allow festering anger to rob you of the intimacy and pleasure every married couple can and should experience.

Stress Leads to Sexual Inhibition

I think it's safe to say we all know that we live in a fast-paced culture. But what not everyone may realize is that one of the most common problems resulting from stress is sexual inhibition. The demands of jobs, children, housework, financial pressures and other issues can leave one or both spouses feeling exhausted and sexually unresponsive. This isn't a problem if it happens infrequently. However, if it happens regularly, it can create deep frustration for the spouse whose sexual needs are being ignored.

So, what's the answer for stress?

The first thing we must do to remove stress from our lives is to prioritize. Regardless of what some people may think, we can't have it all. Life must be prioritized to be successful, and every priority must be protected from competing demands.

God created marriage to be the highest priority in life, with the exception of our personal relationship with Him. He expressed this clearly in Genesis 2:24, when He stated that a man would have to leave his father and mother in order to be joined to his wife. This means that the highest priority in life—the bond between a person and his or her parents—must become a lesser priority for the sake of marriage.

In order to keep our marriage healthy, we need to regularly take inventory of our lives. If we want to prevent stress from taking its toll on our key relationships, we need to examine those things that make demands of us physically, emotionally and mentally. If we realize that the greatest priorities of our lives (God, marriage and children) are being robbed of their rightful place by lesser things (friends, work, sports, hobbies, entertainment), we must be willing to reprioritize or even remove the lesser things.

I gave up golf for several years because of this very issue. I have always loved to play golf, but early in my marriage, it became an idol. I would go directly from work to the golf course and then come home exhausted and unwilling to meet Karen's needs. However, I still expected her to serve me and meet my sexual needs. She was deeply resentful. As you can imagine, it became a major issue in our marriage. At the time, giving up golf was a big sacrifice for me, but as I look back, it was a small price to pay for the incredible intimacy my wife and I share today.

It doesn't matter how successful you are at work or how much money you have if you aren't happy at home. If you think about it, you will agree that nothing else in life has the potential to make you as happy or as miserable as your marriage does. Because of this, it is worthy of the highest level of dedication and sacrifice. Make a decision to prioritize your life, knowing that commitment to your marriage is second only to your commitment to God. Make whatever sacrifices or changes are necessary to give your spouse the time and energy he or she deserves.

Another common source of stress is related to children and housework. Any husband who wants to have good sex must be willing to help on the home front. For a man to come home from work, plop down in front of the television and expect his wife to bear the burden of caring for the children, doing all the housework and preparing the meal is unfair. Particularly if he still expects her to come to bed willing to energetically meet his needs.

Regardless of whether a woman works outside the home or at home, a husband needs to let his wife know that he is her partner in every area of life. A wise husband who wants to enjoy good sex will bear the burdens for his wife and allow her to have a time of rest and relaxation before sex. An unwise husband will ignore his wife and refuse to accept responsibility for the home, children, finances or other issues that are causing her stress.

In dealing with the common stresses of life, it is also a good idea for a husband and wife to plan in advance to have sex. This certainly doesn't rule out spontaneous sex. It just means setting aside time to have sex on a regular basis so that both the husband and wife can make their sexual relationship a priority.

When our children were young and Karen and I had many demands on us, that is precisely what we did. We would decide in advance to schedule an evening together, then we would make sure it happened. These were always times of amazing intimacy because we prioritized and planned for them.

Every two or three months, we also would schedule a night or two away at a motel or hotel so that we could be alone together. When I look back on our marriage and how we were able to succeed in our relationship during very busy times, I believe this was a key reason. We didn't let circumstances dictate what we could or couldn't do, but rather, we made being together and enjoying sex a priority—then we made it happen.

Another issue related to stress we need to be aware of is the fact that children are under more stress now than ever, and that directly affects us as parents. Just like adults, many children believe they have to have everything and be everywhere. As wise parents, we must monitor the demands and desires of our children. Even though all of us will have to work and sacrifice for our children, common sense should tell us where proper parameters should be established. God created us to be parents, not chauffeurs. I know of many couples whose relationships have been damaged and even destroyed because of the unrestrained demands of their children.

Deception Brings Destruction

As I have demonstrated, a huge part of Satan's conspiracy code is sexual deception. We are surrounded by it every day, and if we aren't careful, it will infect our thinking and sabotage our relationships.

Case in point: These days a man need not even leave his home to find himself confronted with erotic images from television, movies, magazines and the Internet. Few, if any, of those images will be of real women (can we say Photoshop?), much less consistent with biblical standards of modesty, dignity or truth.

Pornography is Satan's ultimate weapon, specifically designed to destroy men and marriage. It is nothing less than satanic sex education.

Let me reiterate that pornography portrays women as mere objects, not precious human beings with emotional needs. Therefore, when a man views pornography, he is led to believe that "normal women" want sex as much as he does—and in exactly the way he does. This ultimately leads him to conclude that there is something wrong with his wife and that he is being robbed of the sex life he deserves (and could have with one of these fantasy women).

I have seen many men abuse and abandon their wives as a direct result of falling prey to pornography's twisted portrayal of reality. As men, we must realize that pornography is an illusory trap that leads only to deception and bondage.

One reason pornography's portrayal of sex is so bogus is that it is virtually devoid of real intimacy. You see, God has designed sex to be satisfying only when it is infused with intimacy. Intimacy is an inner closeness and depth of relationship that exists between two *people*— body, soul and spirit—not two *bodies*. In contrast, pornography's portrayal of sex ignores every other area of life and existence, promising sexual fulfillment solely on a physical level. This is the essence of the lie of pornography.

Countless men have destroyed their lives in the pursuit of a mirage—the illusion of sexual fulfillment in the absence of true intimacy. They are driven to constantly feed the monster of sexual excitement, but with ever-diminishing levels of satisfaction. But men are not the only ones vulnerable to deception regarding sex and intimacy.

Romance novels, soap operas, movies, Internet chat rooms, websites, and soft-core female erotica all court a woman's differing sexual temperament. For a woman, these are no less a form of satanic sex education than explicit pornography is for a man. They excite women by downplaying the sexual nature of men and over-emotionalizing them, ignoring the sexual intensity of men.

The worst result of romance novels and female erotica is that they convince women that there are men out there (unlike their husbands) who are much more emotional and much less sexual. That erroneous perception many times causes wives to judge and reject their husbands, as deceived women become convinced they are losing out on "true love."

Reject the lies of the devil and refuse to be entertained or excited by these traps. Then embrace the truth about sex: It is fulfilling for a married couple only as they both turn their hearts to each other and work to meet each other's very different needs.

CHAPTER 26

key #3:
creating an atmosphere conducive to sexual pleasure

Once you understand the differences between you and your spouse, and learn how to overcome the common obstacles to sexual fulfillment, you can pursue unhindered sexual pleasure as a couple. This is one of the greatest blessings of life and marriage. We are sexual beings, and without a doubt, sex is the greatest physical pleasure in life. As I shared earlier, God created marriage in a paradise called "Eden," meaning "pleasure and delights." In doing so, God clearly revealed His design and desire for marriage: Marriage should be a place of sexual pleasure and delight for both husband and wife.

Even though virtually every married couple engages in sexual intercourse, not every couple experiences the same level or frequency of pleasure. Couples can greatly enhance the degree of sexual pleasure in their marriages by creating a relaxed, sensual atmosphere.

Good Health and Proper Grooming

When it comes to our bodies and sex, we encounter two dangerous extremes in our society today. One extreme is the drive for physical perfection, which inspires many people to go to unhealthy extremes in their quest to become more attractive. This obsession with physical appearance means more people are placing unrealistic physical demands on their spouses. For instance, I recently counseled a couple who were separated and on the verge of divorce. The husband constantly criticized his wife for her weight. Not only were his standards unrealistic, he also constantly compared her body to those of models in magazines and actresses on television. As a result, this wife felt rejected and sad.

The second extreme consists in any given individual's abuse of his or her health, without any regard for how it affects his or her spouse and their sexual relationship. Whether heavy drinking, drug abuse or obesity, abuse of the body directly affects our sexuality and our marriages. Why? Because sexual performance is tied directly to our health and well-being (and the older we get, the more true this is). Therefore, each of us must accept responsibility and take care of our physical body.

In addition to maintaining good health, we must also make an effort to practice good hygiene and grooming. Let's be honest: None of us is attracted to people who haven't showered recently!

What does this mean practically speaking? For a man, it means he should be sure that he is clean (read: showered in the previous 12 hours). Also, trimming nose hair and ear hair, having clean teeth and good breath, using cologne, being clean-shaven and dressing well are all important factors. If we want our wives to be attracted to us and open themselves up to us sexually, we must understand how important it is to them that we care for ourselves. To our wives, the way we groom ourselves is a true measure of how much we care about them—and how much we are willing to invest into the relationship.

For a woman, grooming means that she cares for her hair, dress and overall appearance. And most women want to look good for their spouses. In fact, it's usually the case that a woman is taking her husband for granted if she let's herself go. I know of one woman who dramatically dropped the standard of her appearance after her wedding. Prior to saying "I do," she had always looked attractive and well groomed. But immediately after the honeymoon, she "fell apart." Since men are visually stimulated, her disregard for her appearance was her way of saying that she was not concerned with meeting her husband's needs.

Poor grooming and improper hygiene create a negative sexual environment. On the other hand, good health and an attractive appearance go a long way to fostering a positive sexual atmosphere.

Clear Communication

Clear communication is a second critical ingredient for creating a sexually fulfilling atmosphere. The only way we can truly know how to please our spouse sexually is for him or her to tell us. This can and should happen before, during and after sex. This type of open, honest communication happens as we both commit to sharing and to receiving what is shared, in an atmosphere in which each of us feels comfortable giving voice to our sexual needs and desires without risk of being rejected or condemned.

Obviously, if our spouse shares something with us that is sinful or violates our conscience, we don't have to agree to it. However, even then we must be careful how we respond. We need to let our spouse know that we still love him or her and are committed sexually. Typically a man may want his wife to participate in something she may feel violates her. It is important for a woman to be true to her conscience without damaging the relationship or communicating rejection to her husband.

On the other hand, many times a man will become frustrated with his wife because she only communicates with him sexually through negatives. In other words, rather than openly sharing her desires and what pleases her, his wife reserves her sexual comments for when he is doing something wrong. "Stop!" "Don't do that!" "That hurts!" "I don't like that!" When those kinds of comments are the only instructions a man receives in the bedroom, not only is the experience frustrating, but it is also confusing and counterproductive.

Almost every man I know really wants to please his wife sexually (which is not to say men don't have their own set of problems). But husbands depend on positive instruction to succeed. This kind of communication is especially important because men and women are so different in their emotional and physical design and desires.

It is important to note here that a common hindrance to such communication is a repressed attitude toward sex on the part of one of the partners (often the woman). Such an unhealthy attitude is usually communicated through a parent's sexual comments and attitudes. If parents view sex in a negative light, they will normally transmit this directly or indirectly to their children. This negative attitude then profoundly affects that child's future sexual relationship with his or her spouse.

I must emphasize once again that it is God who created sex and that it is beautiful in His eyes. God's perfect will is for you to have a pleasurable, exciting sex life with your spouse. Don't be ashamed of sex or treat it as a taboo issue. Talk about your sexual desires, and encourage your spouse to do the same. Don't let the devil rob you of the joy of sex.

Viewing sex in a negative light because of past sexual sin is also a hindrance to sexual fulfillment. If you've done something wrong, then repent and receive God's forgiveness. But don't let the mistakes of your past keep you from enjoying your sexual life today. Sex, just like anything else, can be good or bad. If you've made mistakes, then use your past as a reminder of what you shouldn't do.

Another issue that affects sexual intimacy in marriage is the issue of past sexual abuse. Perhaps you have experienced sexual abuse at some point in your life. Unless you reveal the sexual abuse to the Lord and allow Him to heal you, your sexual health and marriage will be negatively impacted. It is imperative that you get help if necessary and deal with previous abuse if it is keeping you from opening yourself to sexual pleasure in marriage. Remember, there is nothing that God can't heal or give you the power to overcome.

Be Creative and Energetic in Pleasing Your Spouse

God created sex for two reasons: First, He wants us to procreate; and second, He wants us to experience pleasure in marriage. As we pursue giving and receiving pleasure in marriage, we need to feel free to explore the realms of sexual pleasure and to know where the boundaries are.

As I've taught and counseled on the subject of sex in marriage over the years, I have had many people ask me privately about what is allowed and not allowed sexually. In many cases, couples feel somewhat reluctant to experiment with certain things because they fear they will sin.

Here are some of the common issues people ask me about:

- oral sex
- vibrators and sex toys
- different sexual positions other than the missionary position
- anal sex
- acting out sexual fantasies

In addressing these issues with couples, I first of all tell them that God wants them to enjoy sex. Also, I tell them that when something isn't specifically forbidden in Scripture, it means that it is generally allowed. An example is oral sex. I've heard a good number of preachers over the years talk about how oral sex is a sin. However, Scripture does not forbid it. The same guidelines apply to the other practices listed above. Although I am not necessarily endorsing or recommending any particular practice, I don't believe a preacher or anyone else has the moral authority to decide what a husband and wife can or cannot do in the privacy of their bedroom if the Bible hasn't forbidden it.

Here are some important questions I believe you need to ask yourself when considering a specific sexual practice:

- Is it forbidden in the Bible?
- Does it violate my conscience before God?
- Does it violate my spouse, or is it against his or her will?
- Is this physically safe? Does it cause harm to me or my spouse? Does it involve health risks?
- Does this treat my spouse in a disrespectful manner or damage our relationship?

These are important questions to consider in helping you and your spouse develop sexual parameters. I believe that if something feels good to you and your spouse, and it isn't forbidden in God's Word, you should consider it. The best marriages are those in which two people enjoy each other and make each other feel good. It is important that you approach sex from this perspective and not let the opinions of others dictate your sexual practices. You know better than anyone, except God, what you like and what is best for your marriage. When properly practiced, sex deepens your relationship.

Once you know how to resolve questions related to your sexual practices, it is important to put energy into pleasing your spouse. Remember, if men and women could fulfill themselves sexually, they wouldn't get married. Couples depend upon the creativity and energy of their spouse to meet their sexual needs. Even if they don't understand their spouse's sexual needs, it's important to value those needs. This principle comes into play in marriage when one spouse will have a desire for sex at times when the other doesn't. The temptation for the "non-inspired" spouse is to refuse these advances or to reluctantly participate—which can cause deep frustration and resentment. Each spouse must be sensitive to the needs of the other—and put those needs before his or her own.

Never get lazy or take your spouse for granted. Find out what pleases him or her, and learn to give your spouse sexual pleasure. The more you put into it, the more your marriage will benefit.

Find Positive Solutions to Sexual Problems

Some seasons in marriage bring with them special challenges. For example, normally when a woman enters her late 30s and early 40s, her vaginal lubrication during sex begins to diminish. Because of this, she can experience pain during sex. If the problem isn't addressed, a woman can begin to resist the sexual advances of her husband and actually dread sex. The answer to this issue is for a husband to use a water-based lubricant during intercourse or in direct stimulation of his wife's clitoris. It replaces a woman's natural lubrication and restores the pleasure of sex.

As a man ages, he can begin having difficulty achieving erections. This is obviously a serious problem, but with all of the medical help available today, there is no need for sexual dysfunction to keep any man from experiencing good sex for the rest of his life. So, if this problem presents itself, seek the counsel of a reputable physician.

Many other issues can negatively affect our sex lives: the fear of becoming pregnant, pregnancy, menopause, serious illness, or the loss of a loved one. Regardless of what challenges a couple faces, it is important that they face it together and find a solution. When a medical issue is involved, they need to consult a physician. When the issues are emotional or spiritual in nature, a couple should communicate their needs clearly and then seek professional help, if needed, to keep their marriage as healthy as possible.

Remember that even when you and your spouse are facing difficulties, your sexual needs still need to be met. In a healthy marriage, sex is a constant current that ebbs and flows. When that current slows to a standstill for any significant period of time, it must be viewed as a serious problem that requires attention.

A Final Word

I have been pretty frank and practical here, but it is my hope that these keys to sexual fulfillment have helped to thwart the enemy's plan to rob your marriage of the beauty of sex. If you can't remember the specific keys, don't worry. Remember, the bottom line here is that healthy marriages are marked by an attitude of sexual sensitivity and understanding. And healthy couples meet every sexual challenge or problem with an attitude of mutual concern and commitment to do what is best for the relationship.

living in victory in a fallen world

The Fig Leaf Conspiracy is no paranoid fantasy. It is a very real, very destructive plot aimed directly at God's wonderful gift of sexuality. Through it, Satan has launched an all-out offensive, employing his entire arsenal of subversive tactics. He has done this with one purpose in mind: to steal, kill and destroy your relationships and your family.

In response to the serpent's plans to destroy, we must remember that Jesus has said, "I have come that they may have life, and that they may have it more abundantly." Jesus has made a way for us to experience abundant life in every area—including sexuality.

Satan is after nothing less than our lives, our marriages and our families. But, being forewarned is being forearmed. Now you are.

The lies of the enemy have been exposed. His conspiracy code has been cracked. And his methods no longer remain a mystery. What is more, you are now armed with truth, knowledge, insight and practical wisdom about God's plan for sexuality.

Now that the Fig Leaf Conspiracy has been exposed, you are fully equipped to push back the forces of darkness and allow the sweet presence of God to rule and reign in your home. You see, where God's presence is, there is no shame, no hiding, no fear.

Soon your marriage relationship will resemble what Adam and Eve experienced in the Garden—a husband and wife enjoying God's presence and sharing amazing intimacy with one another. Two people, committed to one another for life, fully and joyously embracing the glorious gift of sex. Hiding under fig leaves no more.

acknowledgments

It takes numerous people hour upon hour to complete the publication of a new book. I am truly blessed to have a terrific team of people assisting me. I want to specifically thank David Holland for his willingness and dedication to diligently work with my teachings and capture my heart and passion and transfer it onto paper. To Virgil Lynn—my appreciation for his unmatched creative abilities and graphic excellence. Special thanks to my son, Brent Evans, who diligently serves and leads the ministry of MarriageToday. I am very proud of you as a son, but also as the leader of this important ministry. To Donna Griffin, Kim LaNore and the entire MarriageToday staff—your dedication to excellence is exemplary. To Bill Greig III, Steven Lawson, Mark Weising, Rob Williams, Kim Bangs and the Regal Books team—your hard work and combined efforts on behalf of this project have not gone unnoticed. I am sincerely grateful to you. Finally, special thanks to my precious wife, Karen, whose absolute love and devotion enable me to fulfill the call on my life. You are my best friend.

Discover
MarriageToday

MarriageToday™
with Jimmy&Karen

Founded by Jimmy and Karen Evans, this ministry is called to establish, strengthen, save, and restore family and marriage relationships through a biblical message of healing, restoration, hope and encouragement.

We are committed to providing families with the teaching and tools they need to succeed through our TV broadcast, literature, resources, seminars and the Internet. And through their prayers and giving, dedicated people are joining with us in our mission to change the future of our nation – one home at a time.

Find out more about MarriageToday at *www.marriagetoday.com*.

An Extraordinary Way to Partner – An Amazing Resource for Your Marriage!

You are cordially invited to join a very special group of couples who value the teaching and encourage- **rock**solid *marriage* ment that comes through MarriageToday. Our "Rock Solid Partners" understand the power and importance of rebuilding and restoring marriage in America, and they want to see this ministry continued and expanded.

What qualifies you as a Rock Solid Partner? A pledge of monthly support to help MarriageToday renew, restore, and repair marriages across America.

The numerous benefits of becoming a partner include a free subscription to the amazing monthly resource we call "Rock Solid Marriage." Each month you'll receive the audio CD with support materials created exclusively for our Rock Solid Partners.

To find out more about how you can receive this exclusive offer, call, write, or click....

MarriageToday™
PO Box 59888, Dallas, TX 75229
1-800-868-8349 —www.marriagetoday.com

Did you know that sex is the covenant sign and seal for marriage? That sexual intimacy is part of God's perfect design for a married couple?

In this timely teaching taken from Genesis 3, relationship expert Jimmy Evans discloses Satan's lies and schemes to distort God's beautiful plan for sexual expression within marriage.

This series will also:

- Outline the importance of sanctifying sex within the marriage relationship
- Bring insight regarding adultery and the spirit behind it
- Refute common and current misconceptions about sex
- Reveal the steps to walk free from shame and sexual sin

Fig Leaf Conspiracy
CD and DVD Series

Is it possible to have the marriage of your dreams? Absolutely!

These life-changing teachings can turn hurting, disillusioned, and even divorce-bound marriages into the dream marriages that God intended them to be. This multi-purpose series contains powerful and clearly defined biblical principles to help guide and prepare you for some of the most crucial undertakings in your life, family and marriage relationships. Ideal for individual study, pre-marriage or couples counseling, small group discipleship, or churchwide marriage seminars.

Couple's Discussion Guide and DVD Series

Marriage on the Rock resources include:

- MOTR Curriculum Kit
- Small Group Workbook
- Couple's Discussion Guide
- CD
- DVD

MarriageToday™
PO Box 59888, Dallas, TX 75229
1-800-868-8349 —www.marriagetoday.com

Build Your Marriage on a Solid Foundation—Here's How!

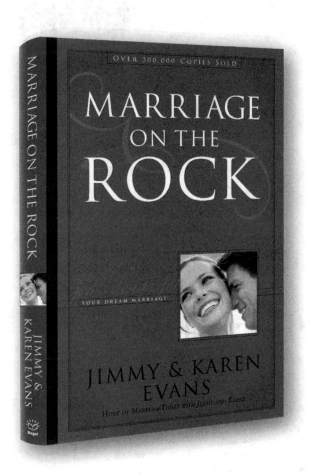

Marriage on the Rock
God's Design for Your Dream Marriage
Jimmy and Karen Evans
ISBN 978.08307.4291

We spend years preparing for our career. But few of us take time to prepare for marriage. Relationship experts Jimmy and Karen Evans invite engaged and married couples to follow some time-tested principles that will help make good marriages stronger, rescue troubled marriages from divorce and help newlyweds get off to a great start.

Learn how good things like children, work, or hobbies can stand in the way of your relationship. Discover who can meet your deepest needs. See what makes a destructive husband or wife. Find out how to make your spouse a priority in your marriage, and how to make time and energy for the two of you. By following the four fundamental laws of marriage Jimmy and Karen Evans outline here, you'll find new peace and satisfaction in your marital relationship, even if you are the only one trying to improve your marriage.

The honeymoon doesn't have to be over! Discover God's design for your dream marriage today.

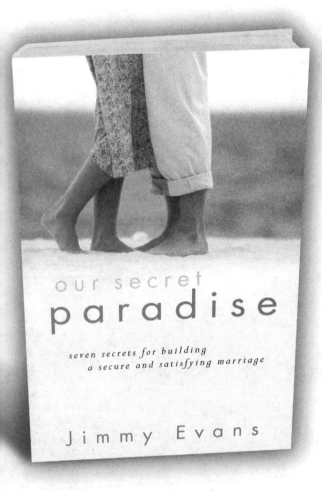